Thinking 101 Learning on the Edge of Chaos

4006 45 Avenue, Bonnyville, Alberta, Canada   T9N 1J4

Geri Lorway B.A., M.ed
Cell: 780-826-1495
Office: 780-826-2231
Email: glorway@telusplanet.net
Web: www.thinking101.ca

So many minds...
So little time

Coming to Know Number:
A Mathematics Activity Resource for Elementary School Teachers

Grayson H. Wheatley
Florida State University

Anne M. Reynolds
University of Oklahoma

Publisher
Mathematics Learning
Tallahassee, Florida
1999

Mathematics Learning
8930 Winged Foot Drive
Tallahassee, FL 32312
Mathlearning@mindspring.com

Third printing,2003

ISBN 1-893799-04-2

Acknowledgements

Just as we argue in this book that students learn mathematics by making sense of their experiences, our epistemology has developed as we have interacted with students, teachers, and scholars. In particular, we have been especially influenced by Leslie Steffe, Paul Cobb, and Erna Yackel. Some of the activities in this book were developed and used in a research project at Purdue University directed by Paul Cobb, Erna Yackel, Terry Wood, and Grayson Wheatley. Many of the ideas reflected in this book were refined in a research project with children at the Florida State University School in Tallahassee, Florida. To the best of our knowledge, the Math Squares activity originated at the Freudenthal Institute in the Netherlands. Bob Wirtz used the Ten Frame idea in a 1980 publication.

To the elementary school teachers who have used these activities and provided comments and suggestions, we give out thanks. We wish to express our deepest appreciation to the children in Florida, Oklahoma, Indiana, North Carolina, Montana, and Michigan who have taught us so much. This book would not have been possible without their involvement. Finally, we would like to than Charlotte Wheatley for her support, many helpful suggestions, and editing.

CONTENTS

Introduction

Since the publication of the NCTM Standards in 1989, mathematics education has been in a period of reform. The NCTM Curriculum and Evaluation Standards suggested new directions in school mathematics curriculum and these recommendations have been taken seriously. Parenthetically, the NCTM Standards are being revised and a new document will be published in April 2000. A clear new direction in school mathematics has emerged, one that has not been ignored by state assessment developers. New tests in states such as Florida, North Carolina, Michigan, and many others now reflect many of the changes recommended by the National Council of Teachers of Mathematics and the reform movement in general.

A conceptual emphasis

A pillar of the reform movement is **a shift from a procedural to a conceptual orientation**. A curriculum that emphasizes computational methods at the expense of mathematics concepts and relationships is no longer acceptable. School mathematics, from kindergarten to the twelfth grade, should have sense making as a central goal. Gone are the days when the teacher explains and students practice computational methods. Also, tubs of manipulatives in centers for students to explore may not be effective - there are important mathematical constructions to target. Instead, students should be engaged in activities that encourage them to construct meaning of big ideas and make sense of their mathematical activity. Instructional materials at each grade level that have this emphasis ARE available. Real reform must be based on what we now know about student learning.

American textbooks have been described as "a mile wide and an inch deep," and our nation's teaching methods have been labeled superficial at best. According to the recent Third International Mathematics and Science Study (TIMSS), "American texts are superficial, peppered with far too many topics and often not offered in an order that makes pedagogical sense. Mathematics textbooks are as splintered as the system itself. American textbooks are major obstacles to higher levels of academic performance by American students. The goal is not merely textbooks with fewer topics, or even lengthier treatment of 'key' topics, but books with a coherent vision of the disciplines presented as an unfolding story, allowing even children in the early grades to connect bits and pieces to larger

1

concepts. . . . Current textbooks available in most American classrooms remain superficial, despite the drive toward national and state standards and assessments." (Schmidt, McKnight and Raizen, 1997).

What is mathematics?

Mathematics is constructing patterns and relationships

While many persons see education as the process of acquiring knowledge that involves memorizing facts and procedures, mathematics is not just a set of rules. An alternative way of thinking about mathematics is as the activity of constructing patterns and relationships. In this view, mathematics is something people do. Knowledge is not acquired but constructed by the individual as he or she solves problems. In today's fast changing society with numerous new challenges, it is important that students give meaning to mathematical activity and be able to solve problems not seen previously.

Mathematics is reasoning, not memorization. While it is useful to know certain facts and procedures, it is essential that these facts and procedures develop with understanding. For example, a student who thinks in tens can see immediately that 34 + 16 is 50 without going through some arbitrary set of steps by making marks on paper. Mathematics is more like learning to find your way around a park with many trails. With experience which involves exploration, a person can build a mental map of the park and move through the park without ever being lost. In the same way children can build networks of schemes which allow them to cope with novelty and solve problems they have not previously considered. Just memorizing facts and procedures can actually be debilitating. It bypasses the important activity of building inter-connected mathematical ideas.

Instructional materials

Students learn from reorganizing their thinking, not drill

Many instructional materials are based on the belief that teaching is explaining with students practicing specific methods. It is clear that students learn best when they reorganize their thinking as a result of a perturbation and develop their own knowledge as they interact with others. The instructional materials greatly influence the nature of learning that occurs. In reviewing instructional materials, the following questions should be asked:

1) Are the goals and activities conceptual rather than procedural?

2) Are *big ideas* in mathematics apparent and emphasized?
3) Do the activities encourage students to make sense of what they are doing - to become responsible for their own learning?
4) What instructional strategies are utilized?
5) Will the activities enhance mathematics learning?

In this book, you will find many activities that have proven effective in helping children come to know number. Among the activities included are the following:

Dot Patterns

Dot patterns help children develop mental imagery for numbers. Used in a Quick Look" format, they engender thinking in collections which is a precursor to constructing number abstractly. Dot pattern activities using rectangular arrays also is the beginning of multiplicative reasoning.

Ten Frames

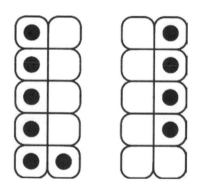

Ten Frames have proven highly effective in helping students think in tens and develop strategies for adding and subtracting. This teacher directed whole class activity encourages students to think of six as a collection and also in relation to ten. Students can make tens in determining the total number of dots seen.

Combo-Ten

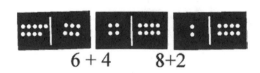

6 + 4   8+2

Combo-Ten illustrates how a game can be a fruitful setting for constructing number relationships, in this case, thinking in tens.

Balances

Balances are a "bread and butter" activity for coming to know number meaningfully. While ini-

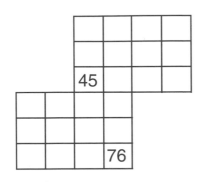

tially students may use counters to determine how many, the balance format encourages students to develop efficient thinking strategies to construct patterns and relationships.

Hundreds Boards

Hundred Board activities encourage children to develop the number sequence with an accent on ten as a building block. As with all the tasks, hundreds boards are just a setting for students to construct patterns and relationships. There is no mathematics, per se, in hundreds boards

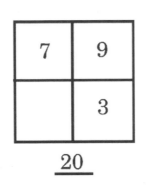

Math Squares

Math Squares provide rich opportunities for students to use tens and refine their thinking strategies in a meaningful setting. They encourage students to consider alternatives in determining what operations to perform next.

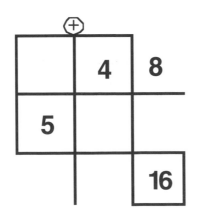

Two Ways

Two Ways help students elaborate mathematics patterns and relationships and further the development of mental arithmetic methods. Their self-checking nature serves students and teachers alike.

Problem Solving

Nonroutine problems are one of the best settings for students to develop mathematical reasoning. Nonroutine problems are not to be confused with the standard word problems in text designed to practice computational skill. A discussion of problem solving can be found in the section of this book by that name. A set of suggested problems for your use are provided.

> I am thinking of a number. If I double it and add 7, I get 19. What is the number?

Based on research and experience in many classrooms, these activities are designed to encourage students to think in tens, develop thinking strategies and their own methods for adding and subtracting whole numbers. Mathematics is a mental activity and number sense is crucial for individuals in the rapidly changing information age. This approach, proven superior in many studies, contrasts with an approach that emphasizes rote memorization of facts and practicing computational algorithms prescribed by the teacher. It also contrasts with an approach that is based on the belief that there is mathematics in manipulatives – that mathematics is out there to be discovered.

A problem centered instructional strategy is described and illustrated. A task is presented, students work in pairs formulating their solution which is then shared with the class. The class functions as an intellectual community in which the students become self-validators rather than depending on the teacher to prescribe and judge. Embedded assessment is recommended with the emphasis on learning rather than frequent testing. The goal of this program is a high level of competency – students who can use their knowledge to solve nonroutine problems as well as perform routine mathematics tasks efficiently. It is also important for students to enjoy mathematics as an intellectual activity.

We hope these activities will greatly enhance your teaching. You can be sure students will enjoy them and gain understanding of number.

Part I

Helping Children Learn Mathematics

Thinking in units

Counting can be over-emphasized

Many factors contribute to a child's construction of number in an abstract sense. Steffe et. al. (1983) present a theory of number development which is based on counting. While students will naturally go through a series of well defined stages in reaching a level of abstract counting, many students come to rely on counting at the expense of constructing important and useful thinking strategies. We are suggesting that activities that encourage counting may be limiting for some students. An approach to early number which emphasizes units rather than counting is the basis for the activities in this book.

For a number of years we have been engaged in research into children's mathematical thinking, particularly their construction of number and the imagery involved in their sense making. Some of these studies have been published (Reynolds and Wheatley, 1996; Wheatley and Reynolds, 1996) . Our research has focused on individual students as well as whole class settings at several age levels. In each case the research is in the tradition of a teaching experiment approach, as elaborated by Steffe (1991), where we have interacted with students over a year or longer as we posed tasks that had the potential to engage them in learning and thus probed their emerging mathematical constructions. In developing our thesis in this book we draw on this research base.

Older students may still rely on counting-on to add 8 + 7

Preliminary investigations suggest that many students, even in middle school, still rely on counting as a primary method of adding. For example, to determine 8 + 7, many (too many) grade seven students will count-on saying, 9, 10, 11, 12, 13, 14, 15. These students seem to have stagnated in their construction of number with an inefficient, procedural method. That is, they have developed neither number relationships nor efficient procedures and obviously have not "memorized" 8 + 7 = 15. Counting dominates their thinking and unfortunately remains their method of finding sums and differences. It also seems that efforts to get students to memorize are not being successful. On the other hand, students who think in collections and use thinking strategies are able to approach both routine and nonroutine mathematics tasks flexibly

9

and effectively (Nicholls, et. al., 1991). When they use thinking strategies, students construct a network of schemes which leads to rapid responses to addition and subtraction situations as well as using relationships they have constructed.

As students enter school, learning to count is one of their central mathematical activities. When students begin determining the total number in two sets they will usually count-all and later move to counting-on. Much is learned through counting. However, an over-reliance on counting rather than number patterns leads many students to continue using counting while others have shifted to more powerful reasoning. In the primary grades there is often a push for students to memorize addition facts. No grade three teacher wants to see students counting to find sums. Teachers work very hard to help students memorize their addition facts. So why are so many students still using counting in grade 7?

While it is recognized that addition and subtraction algorithms taught in school are procedural and may not be meaningful to young students, rarely has counting been viewed in the same way. When students try to learn the subtraction algorithm for subtracting whole numbers, attempting to remember the steps in a teacher demonstrated procedure, they may not give meaning to their activity. In the same way, counting may have little meaning to some students. In an interview setting, Alex (grade one) counted a set of six objects and said there were six. When then asked to solve a problem using the set, he recounted them (in fact, more than once) as he tried to use a counting strategy. He had to "make" the six each time - he had not constructed six as a mathematical object. His counting was a procedure that did not result in taking the set as a collection with numerosity. Wirtz (1980) noted that counting seemed to interrupt the flow of thinking about what was going on. He wrote, ". . . during the time involved in counting one-by-one, the connection between the intention (i. e., comparing dominoes) and the outcome broke down" (p. 3). This is a stinging indictment of counting as the basis for early mathematical activity.

By a collections approach to early number development we mean focusing on student's construction of units (Wheatley and Reynolds, 1996).

Drilling on addition facts is not working

Thinking in collections is a promising alternative

10

A child has developed an abstract concept of number when she has mental imagery associated with a numeral, number word or set of objects and can flexibly use the unit in adding or subtracting and can decompose the unit into singleton units. The development of thinking strategies such as compensation (7 + 9 is 16 because 8 + 8 =16; taking one from nine is compensated for by putting one with seven) is enhanced by thinking in units. In a collections approach, students may at first only form static images but as they continue constructing number, this image can become dynamic and quite useful. As children experience fourness in many settings they can abstract four from the particular objects or picture seen and their knowing becomes operational.

A student has constructed four as a mathematical object when the unit (four) simultaneously is four separate units and one unit. Counting does not encourage this construction since it is a sequential activity and the last word said is the name of the abstract number; there is a tendency for students to think only of the single objects and not "make" the collection. Tammy, a third grade student, was so routinized to counting that she could not give meaning to number abstractly. She would look at a domino and count the dots rather than knowing the number based on the pattern. It was as if the collection did not exist, only the single dots. Megan, a fifth grader who had been taught using Touch Math in which points on numerals are counted in adding and subtracting, had made little sense of numbers and could not function in a grade five mathematics class. Her counting-on using points on numerals was very fast and efficient. In fact, it was so efficient that she did not feel the need to develop another method of adding in the school mathematics settings. Counting seemed to block her sense making. On the other hand, Adam, a first grader, could deal meaningfully with arrangements of six or seven dots even though his response to 3 + 1 = was to haltingly count-all. Adam had developed a collections scheme of number. By this we mean he could take six as a unit composed of units. Such a scheme can become the basis for his additive thinking as the activities in this book demonstrate.

Susan Shellcock at Dickson Elementary School frequently used an activity she called Spot-

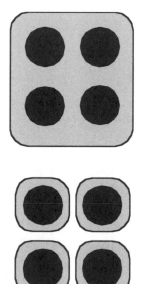

Spot-the-Dot

11

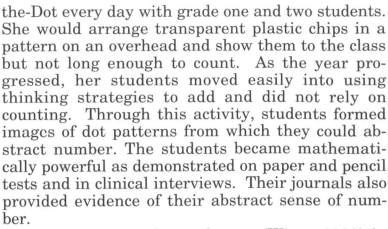

the-Dot every day with grade one and two students. She would arrange transparent plastic chips in a pattern on an overhead and show them to the class but not long enough to count. As the year progressed, her students moved easily into using thinking strategies to add and did not rely on counting. Through this activity, students formed images of dot patterns from which they could abstract number. The students became mathematically powerful as demonstrated on paper and pencil tests and in clinical interviews. Their journals also provided evidence of their abstract sense of number.

Activities with ten frames (Wirtz, 1980) in which some dots in a 5 by 2 grid are shown briefly on the overhead and students are asked to say how many they saw, encourage thinking in collections rather than counting. Through use of this activity students come to think in units rather than just sequentially saying number names. In Norman, Oklahoma a grade two class used ten frames extensively along with other activities (Wheatley, 1996) which encourage the use of imagery and showed evidence of thinking in collections. For example, two ten frames were shown briefly on an overhead projector. The following transcript indicates how students transformed an image of dot patterns in determining the total number of dots.

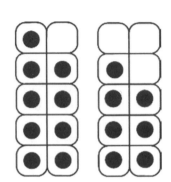

Marta: "I took those over to those" (indicating the 3 dots at the top of columns in the left ten frame, which she mentally 'moved' to fill the right ten frame).

Teacher: "Why?"

Marta: "Because if you do that you got six left and ten on that side."

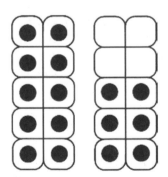

Katie: "I saw four empty boxes; I knew that 20 minus 4 would be 16."

Cole: "I saw 4 and 4 and 4 and 3 and 1 (meaning 4s arranged as 2 rows of two dots, starting with the left ten frame seeing four at the bottom and another four above that, then the right ten frame with four at the bottom, then the remaining 3 on the right and 1 on the left)."

The examples above show the different ways students determined the total number of dots. Marta transformed her image of the ten frames by moving dots from the left ten frame to the right with the intention of making a ten. She was then able to use her knowledge of our numeration system to combine six and ten to make 16. Cole decomposed the collection into manageable units that he could combine. Katie used an even more sophisticated strategy involving complements. Knowing there were 20 spaces in the two ten frames, she took the number of empty spaces as a mathematical object (4) and was able to formulate the subtraction task, 20 - 4, and determine the difference to be 16. She just knew 20 - 4 = 16. In each case, there was evidence of students thinking in collections that they could transform rather than relying on rote counting.

These students were reasoning with numbers without relying on any procedure such as counting. This activity of mentally transforming dots in ten frames led to use of thinking strategies in addition. For example, on another day in determining 9 + 7, Marta said she made the 9 into 10 by moving 1 from the 7 to the 9 so that it was 10 and 6. There was no need of her to count on from 9 by ones as so many middle grades students still do. We also contend this way of thinking about addition is superior to just memorizing facts - they are giving meaning to their activity. As the students continue to do addition problems in this manner, they come to know their addition combinations without drill and timed tests. Wirtz (1980) observed that the children enjoyed 'pushing the dots around in their heads.' Wheatley and Reynolds (1996) provide evidence for the power of mental transformations of images as children construct number concepts.

Imaging that is initially based on figural patterns of objects can be useful to children in constructing number in a meaningful way - a way that leads to using powerful thinking strategies for adding and subtracting. Grade one and even younger students can learn to associate a number name with a pattern of dots and subsequently use this figural material in a process of reflective abstraction to construct number (von Glasersfeld, 1987, p. 297). Hatano (1979) developed a successful system of early arithmetic instruction based ini-

Using thinking strategies

Having mental imagines for numbers is helpful

13

tially on figural patterns from which students developed number relationships. In commenting on a collections approach, Wirtz (1980) wrote, "When they become more involved with written symbols, those symbols will have a deeply ingrained referent in the experience of the learners." (p. 5)

Through activities with dot patterns, ten frames and other tasks that encourage thinking in collections, young students construct an abstract concept of number without resorting to a procedure to "make" the number each time by counting. Of course, the collections approach in which a child can mentally transform a set to a familiar pattern for which a number name is known, depends on conservation of number (Piaget, 1952). But to encourage counting can actually interfere with the construction of number in that it is a rote process that may be devoid of any mathematical meaning. This is not to say that counting cannot be meaningful but that for many students it becomes a substitute for sense making.

Summary

We are suggesting that a collections approach to number can be more effective than attempting to build mathematics on counting. Students will always count and it is a useful procedure. However, students who rely heavily on counting in computing and problem solving may not be constructing essential mathematical relationships necessary for success in more demanding mathematics tasks.

While counting is an important component of acting mathematically and students may make important mathematical constructions by curtailing their counting activity, there is the real danger they will come to rely on this procedure as a method for getting answers without reflecting on their activity. Tasks that encourage students to think in collections provide rich opportunities for them to construct abstract mathematical relationships and become powerful problem solvers. Rather than viewing counting as the basis for number constructions, we present evidence that a collections approach that encourages the construction of units may be more effective.

Children build mental images of dot patterns that become the material for abstracting number. Thinking in collections and using thinking strategies paves the way for quantitative reasoning. As

Thinking in collections leads to mathematical power

14

Smith (1997) states, "But an explicit focus on quantity and quantitative reasoning is an important instructional goal, co-equal to the focus on number and operation. Students' capacity to reason about quantities and their relationships is a major factor influencing their ability to think about physical situations and solve problems, including but not limited to the word problems commonly found in the current school curriculum." (p.23) The collections approach leads naturally to quantitative reasoning as expressed by Smith.

Constructing Ten as an Abstract Unit

Constructing ten as an abstract composite unit is central to using number meaningfully. There are many levels in constructing abstract number units. A child may count six objects, saying "one, two, three, four, five, six" without taking the collection of objects as a mathematical entity. That is, they are counting single objects and that is the only unit constructed. At a second level, the child may count as before but take six as a collection. However, the set is either one thing (the set), or six things (six separate units) and for the child the two conceptualizations are unrelated. At a third level the child can coordinate the set and the separate objects. In this case we say the child has constructed six as an abstract composite unit. It is composite because the child can *simultaneously* think of one thing and six things. Thus the child at this level can mentally combine sets to make six and decompose six into subunits.

Ten, the base of our numeration system is a special number and it is important that students learn to think in tens. An important milestone in a child's mathematical thinking is reached when she or he constructs ten as a composite unit, that is, can think of ten as one thing or ten things simultaneously. At a still higher level, a child may construct ten as an iterable unit which means that he or she can know that ten more than 37 is 47. This action requires knowing that 47 is ten ones more than 37 as well as one ten more. Unitizing plays a major role in much of number development. Constructing abstract units is essential not only in addition and subtraction but for nearly all mathematical topics such as multiplication, fractions, decimals, percents and proportions.

Cobb and Wheatley (1988) investigated second grade students' initial understandings of ten as they completed tasks involving incrementing and decrementing by tens and ones. There was evidence, which agreed with the findings of Steffe (1983), that the unitizing operation was central in the construction of ten as a mathematical entitiy and in the whole number sequence in general. Students constructed ten as an abstract unit at several levels. At the first level, ten was constructed as a numerical composite in which the meaning given to the set was as ten ones or a single

entity but it was not both simultaneously. The child may be able to distinguish those items that can be counted using the sequence 10, 20, 30,..... (ten as an abstract singleton) from those to be counted using the standard number word sequence but does not see one ten as composed of ten ones. At the second level ten was constructed as an abstract composite unit when ten could be taken as a single entity while maintaining its tenness. Finally ten became for the child an iterable unit where the unit of ten could be used to "measure out" tens as in adding ten to 37 to get 47.

Ten is a special number because of the nature of our numeration system that is based on ten, perhaps because we have ten fingers. It is important for students to learn to think in tens, to form the intention to make a ten. For most of us, it is not possible to look at a set of objects and just know there are ten as we could with a set of five or six. However, we can determine there are ten there by mentally forming the objects into smaller units such as four, four and two. This act of decomposing the set into sub-units is useful, not just in determining how many objects in a set, but in adding and subtracting. To add 7 + 5 a student might break the 5 into 3 and 2, combine the 7 and 3 to make ten and then put the 2 with 10 to make 12. Or in 13 − 8, the student may first take away 3, to make a ten, and then 5. Initially this action is possible if the student has constructed ten as an abstract unit and anticipated, before acting, that he or she will make a ten. Ten has become a benchmark number, a mathematical entitiy which is simultaneously one thing and ten things; it can be taken as a whole (not a one) or decomposed into sub-units.

Students are in a position to develop powerful methods for adding and subtracting large numbers when they have constructed ten as an abstract unit. For example, in adding 37 and 29, a student who has constructed ten as an abstract unit (and who has not been required to use particular procedures) may use ten as a benchmark, moving one from 37 to 29 to make 30 (three tens) and then easily combine 36 and 30 to get 66. Students who have to count on or use a memorized paper-pencil algorithm will be at a disadvantage as mathematics gets more complex. They begin to see these strategies as not being efficient: "This is way too slow!"

or "I lost my place and I have to count over." At the same time, it should be noted that simply providing larger numbers (like 37 + 29) is often not sufficient for some students, in encouraging the construction of ten as an abstract unit. We have all seen students who will happily, day after day, get out a box of counters, and tediously count out the numbers in ones, without challenging themselves to refine their methods. At the same time, we need to be using other tasks that encourage students to image ten as a collection to help them develop more efficient procedures for adding and subtracting. This can be done through the astute use of appropriate classroom openers as described in this book. We also need to provide many earlier experiences that will encourage children to "make tens" as they develop thinking strategies.

Activities that provide opportunities for students to construct ten as an abstract unit include:

Quick Dot
Ten Frames
Combo-Tens
Ten Frame Match
Balances
Hundreds Boards
Math Squares
Two Ways
Money

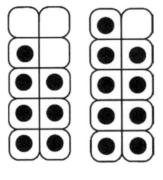

For example, when shown a double ten frame, several first grade students responded:

Katie: I took the three from the top of the right frame and put it with the seven to make ten. I had to turn it to fit it in. So ten and six make sixteen.

Paul: I saw there was one missing (in the right ten frame) so I took one from the seven to make that ten. Then I had ten and six.

Phil: I saw four and another four and one (on the right ten frame) and a one from the other side makes ten.

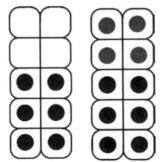

Sara: I saw six on the bottom and another six on the bottom and the four left over. So six and four makes ten and six is sixteen.

Katie and Paul both anticipated making ten as an easy way of thinking about how many dots they saw. They used the ten frame to help them think about how many dots they needed to "move" from one frame to the other to make ten, believing that once they made a ten, they could easily add in the number that was left over. Katie mentally turned the three dots she saw on the top of the right ten frame to fill in the left ten frame. Paul saw "there was one missing," which meant that there were nine in the right frame. He could reduce the seven in the left frame by one to make his ten on the right. Phil also anticipated making a ten on the right but he did not immediately "see" as Paul had that there were nine in this frame. He constructed the nine by thinking of a collection of four and another collection of four and one more. Sara's thinking was somewhat different. She initially organized her dots into two collections of six dots, one from each frame and a collection of four dots (the three remaining on the left and the one on the right), with one remaining. However, faced with the need to combine 6 and 6 and 4, she reorganized her collections so as to make a ten by combining 6 and 4.

A major focus in the primary grades should be providing a variety of experiences that promote the construction of ten as an abstract unit. As teachers we cannot make this construction for our students; nor can we "show" them how our number system works. Students must do this themselves in their own meaningful ways. Our role as teacher is to anticipate student's needs to struggle with this idea and to provide various and long-term challenges so they have the opportunity and support they need to make this leap.

Thinking Strategies

Mathematics is a creative activity.

Mathematics in the elementary school often has computation as a focus. Even though national and state guidelines suggest a broadening of the mathematics curriculum, many educators and parents cling to the belief that mathematics is about becoming skillful at performing paper and pencil computations rapidly, so that it can be done without thought. A different perspective considers mathematics to be a creative activity in which students are constructing patterns and relationships.

Emphasis should be on making sense.

With the advent of inexpensive calculators and computers, the need for high levels of proficiency with complex computations such as multi-digit long division has diminished. On the other hand, estimation and mental arithmetic have assumed more central roles. A goal of school mathematics should be the development of an interrelated web of meanings which allow a person to move around easily in the world of mathematics; to approach tasks in a variety of ways. This suggests that the elementary school mathematics curriculum should place emphasis on making sense of mathematics relationships and being able to reason flexibly. Thinking strategies as described below should be central to the mathematics curriculum.

Thinking Strategies:
  Double + 1
  Making ten
  Compensation

Thinking strategies are one way we can encourage students to build fundamental relationships and develop efficient ways of adding. For example, many students find it easy to learn doubles because of symmetry. Knowing doubles can be a basis for solving many problems by converting a task to one involving doubles. A student might find 6 + 7 by thinking 6 + 6 and one more. This is called the **doubles-plus-one** thinking strategy. A doubles minus one thinking strategy is equally useful.

When considering 9 + 7, students have a variety of ways of determining the sum. **Making Ten** is one thinking strategy that has proven to be quite powerful. Using this thinking strategy, a student might reason that by taking one from seven and putting it with the nine, the task is changed to 10 + 6 which can then be seen as 16. A student who uses this method has obviously constructed ten as an abstract unit and forms the intention of making ten. Thus, for such students, ten has become a benchmark number that has special significance. If a student has not constructed ten as a mathematical object, she or he will not see this strategy as a

Ten becomes a benchmark number.

possibility and may instead, have to count-on or rely on a memorized fact that may have little meaning.

Another thinking strategy is **compensation**. The task considered in the paragraph above, 9 + 7 could be solved by "moving" one from nine to the seven making 8 + 8. Since many students know their doubles, 16 can be determined. This strategy is called compensation because taking one from the nine is compensated for by adding one to the seven. In a similar manner, a student might determine 23 + 17 by shifting three from 23 to 17 making 20 + 20, which can then easily be renamed as 40.

Self-generated algorithms

Typically, a particular method of adding or subtracting is demonstrated and students are instructed to use this textbook method, which is then practiced over and over. The focus is on becoming proficient in using this particular skill. Unfortunately, many students do not understand what they are doing and their activity is mechanical. The set of algorithmic steps are often performed with no thought to the meaning involved. An alternative is to encourage students to develop their own methods that make sense to them. These are referred to as self-generated methods. Actually it might be better to think of them as evolving from class interactions as well as individual thought. Shown below are examples of student generated methods for adding and subtracting using thinking strategies.

32 + 9 =

Laurie: Use 8 from 9 to make 40, leaving 1 which is then added to 40 to get 41.

Randy: Counts on by tens: 32, 42, then back off one . . .41.

34 - 7 =

Nancy: Treats 34 as 30 and 4, 30 - 7 is 23, now add the 4 which is 27.

Beca: Subtracting in parts; 34 - 4 is 30, 30 - 3 is 27.

Bobbi: Adding 3 to make a convenient 37; $37 - 7 = 30$, now subtract the 3 which was added yielding 27.

$$\begin{array}{r} 29 \\ + 58 \\ \hline \end{array}$$

Val: Takes 1 from 8 to put with the 9 to make 10, 50 + 20 + 10 is 80, 80 + 7 (7 left) is 87.

Sarah: 30 + 58 is 88, one less is 87.

Patti: 70 + 17 is 87.

Dan: Counting up from 58 - - 68, 78, 87.

$$\begin{array}{r} 74 \\ - 28 \\ \hline \end{array}$$

Kim: Subtracting 20 from 70 which is 50, subtract 8 from 4 which is four in the hole so subtract 4 from 50. . . 46.

Joanne: Add 4 at the beginning and subtract it out at the end; 74 + 4 is 78, 78 − 28 = 50, now subtract 4, 46.

Katie: 74 - 24 is 50 now subtract the remaining 4.

Examples of children's thinking

When faced with a task requiring computation, many elementary school students act mechanically using poorly understood procedures rather than meaning-based reasoning. The following two examples illustrate what can happen if procedures are the focus of the mathematics curriculum.

Addi, a grade three student, was asked "What is twenty-one take away nineteen?" Her response was to perform the traditional subtraction algorithm on her "mental blackboard." After "borrowing" a one from the two to make 11, she reported a two under the 9 and a 0 under the 1.

$$\begin{array}{r} \overset{1}{2}\overset{11}{1} \\ -1\,9 \\ \hline 0\,2 \end{array}$$

She did not actually give an answer to the question but considered her task finished when she had carried out the procedure. The numbers had no numerical value but were just symbols to be manipulated according to fixed rules.

When Jack, also a third grader was asked the same question, "twenty-one take away nineteen" he counted back by ones nineteen times from twenty-one to get two. At least he answered the question even though he used a laborious method that might be impossible with larger numbers. Neither of these students seemed to give meaning to 19 and 21 in a number sequence. Each of these examples, in different ways, show the result of imposing procedures, emphasizing counting and memorizing without opportunities to make sense of mathematics.

Mathematical reasoning is an important goal

In contrast, Ryan, a third grader, when asked the same question responded "two" immediately, indicating that he just counted up from 19 to 21 and found two counts. During the previous school year, Ryan had been in a class where he was encouraged to give meaning to his mathematical experiences and develop his own ways of thinking with numbers. In this environment, Ryan had developed a variety of meaningful methods for adding and subtracting numbers.

Conventional mathematics instruction in the elementary school has memorization and "mastery" of specific procedures as goals. While some students make sense of numbers and learn to compute using procedures prescribed by the teacher, many students fail to understand what they are doing, become frustrated, anxious and turn away from mathematics because it does not make sense to them. The examples above show why a shift from procedures to reasoning is essential.

Which Route Will You Follow?

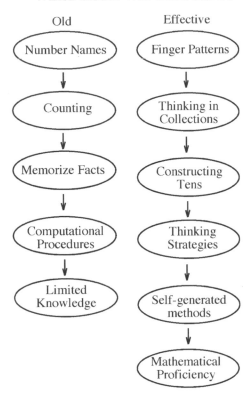

The diagram above shows two paths that can be followed in teaching number. On the left is the traditional method whereby emphasis is on memorization of facts followed by practice on teacher demonstrated computational procedures. Little attention is given to the meaning of the operations of addition and subtraction while speed and accuracy with computation is the goal. On the right is an alternative that has proven effective. In this route students are encouraged to give meaning to their activity and develop quantitative reasoning. If students learn to think in collections rather than relying on counting and learn to think in tens then they are in a position to develop facility with computation using methods they develop. Students are not working in isolation — there is much sharing of number patterns and computational methods. In this way students construct a network of meanings that they can use in new settings. They learn to think mathematically.

The Basic Facts Issue

We have thought deeply about the question of memorizing facts and have spent hours interviewing students about their knowledge of arithmetic operations and procedures. First, it is important that students come to know the addition and multiplication facts. The question is, "How do students become knowledgeable in using these operations?"

Our research over the past 20 years shows that early memorization of facts is detrimental and timed tests do more harm than good. This may seem like a strong statement and be at odds with conventional instruction but we have data to support it. Many middle school students count-on in determining 8 + 7. It is important that students understand numbers and be able to use their knowledge to solve problems. Early focus on memorizing addition facts detracts from students constructing their knowledge of addition and subtraction. Obviously, the efforts of teachers to get these students to memorize facts in isolations were not effective.

In order to become mathematically powerful, students must develop number sense, which includes many patterns and relationships among numbers. When students are forced to memorize, it short circuits learning - they may associate 15 with 7 and 8 without any idea what it means. Furthermore, they come to believe they are not supposed to make sense of mathematics but just memorize it like a set of strange characters. In today's world, memorized facts alone do not get us very far.

An alternative to memorization is a set of meaningful activities that encourage students to construct patterns and relationships. For example, students have little difficulty knowing their doubles. They use thinking strategies such as "6+ 7 is 13 because 6 and 6 is 12 and one more is 13." Another thinking strategy students will use if they have constructed 10 as an abstract unit is 7 + 5 = 12 because 7 and 3 is 10, 10 and 2 is 12. When students are engaged in meaningful activities such as Ten Frames and Balances, there are many opportunities for them to build their knowledge in a way that will be useful to them is doing mathematics.

The usual path to number computation is: learn number names, counting, memorize facts, then memorize a procedure for computing. An al-

Memorization can short circuit learning

Mathematics is the activity of constructing patterns and relationships

ternative path that leads to mathematical power is thinking in collections (dot patterns, ten frames), ten as an abstract unit, thinking strategies, then self-generated algorithms. The latter approach has proven more effective (Nicholls, Cobb, Yackel, Wood, Wheatley, Trigatti, and Perlwitz, 1991).

Grade three is too early to drill students on multiplication facts but multiplication should be a central topic. During grades four and five as multiplication is continued to be studied, it would be appropriate from time to time to have students take inventory of those facts they do not know or have difficulty figuring out with encouragement to use activities to construct them. This must not get in the way of understanding multiplication. The best way to come to know multiplication is much work on mental math and doing lots of multiplication in meaningful settings.

In summary, mathematics is more than computation and while it is important for students to know their facts (have efficient methods), rote memorization does not encourage the view of mathematics needed for this information age. Mathematics is more than computation. If we immerse students in rich activities that encourage sense making, students will develop efficient methods for computing. Memorization of addition facts in grade one and times tables in grade three is counter productive.

Manipulatives

In the movie "Searching for Bobby Fischer" the chess teacher places a few pieces on the board and asks Josh (seven years old) for the best move. Josh says he "can't see it." The teacher sweeps all the pieces off the board and says, "Don't move until you see it." Josh stares at the blank board for some time and then says, "Now I see it." Sometimes the concrete can get in the way of our thinking.

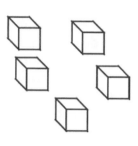

Historically in this country, arithmetic has meant memorizing facts and practicing computational procedures. Granted there have been visionaries such as Dewey, Freudental, and Brownell, still the mathematical experience of most children has been primarily rote and mechanical. During the past twenty years as mathematics education research has matured and theories of learning based on studying children have been formulated, a broader concept of arithmetic has evolved. In fact, few persons even speak of arithmetic but think about mathematics that encompasses much more than computation with numbers.

Too much with us? In the nineties, much is being written about the role of manipulatives in teaching mathematics. Using manipulatives is often taken as a mark of a good mathematics program. Yet manipulative activity can be just as procedural as using a subtraction algorithm. For example, students using the multi-based blocks can be instructed to exchange ten cubes for one ten rod as the teacher explains regrouping. Such teacher directed activity may have little meaning for the young students. To a person who has already constructed ten as an abstract composite unit, the exchange makes sense. However, it may not do much for the child who is still counting-all in adding numbers. There is no mathematics in the blocks. Having students move three blocks and then two blocks may not be seen as addition to a first grader even if she is told it is and she writes 3 + 2 = 5. As teachers, there is a tendency to believe students experience objects the same as we do.

Manipulatives such as Multilink cubes can be quite useful to students as they construct number relationships. However, extensive use of manipulatives can result in students relying on counting rather than conceptualizing two sets as two collections that make a new collection.

At times, it is better not to have all objects visible. For example, if I hold nine chips in my two hands and then put some in each, showing the right hand containing four chips and ask how many are in the other closed hand, students will need some other method of deciding than counting the objects. If the same question is posed with both sets visible a student can just use a counting procedure which may have little meaning.

So the question is not *whether* manipulatives are used but *how* they are used. In this book, manipulatives are recommended for some of the activities but the emphasis is on mental rather than physical activity. It is crucially important for learners to develop mental ways of reasoning with numbers so they will not need to rely on physical objects. Without this emphasis on mental activity, students may develop procedures for getting answers with manipulatives that may impede the building of number relationships. For example, some students have numberlines on their desks. Students quickly develop a procedure for getting answers using the numberline but may not give meaning to their activity. Touch Math has also been found to retard the development of number concepts because students can just count-on with no thought about what their counting means.

In summary, manipulatives can facilitate the learning of mathematics and do have a place in the math classroom. However, care must be exercised in how they are used. If students develop some primitive procedure for getting answers without thinking, the manipulatives may actually interfere with learning. Once students have developed a way of adding or subtracting with the aid of manipulatives, it is time to ask, "Can you do it without the blocks?" For some students the answer may be no and they should be allowed to continue using the manipulatives, always being encouraged to develop mental ways of adding and subtracting.

How manipulatives are used is the important question

Negotiating Effective Learning Environments in Mathematics Classrooms

As you enter Ms. Diaz' classroom you see Sara and Tom engaged in a heated exchange about the interpretation of a problem they are solving while the other students are solving other problems, also in pairs. Sara says there could be many possible answers while Tom maintains that there is only one. Tyrone and Marta are jointly collaborating in developing a solution, playing off each other's ideas. The teacher is moving around the room being very attentive to the interaction but not becoming too engaged with any group. After 25 minutes, the teacher calls the class together and asks for Sara and Tom to explain their reasoning in the problem they solved. The other students had worked on the same task, perhaps at a different time. As Sara and Tom explain their solution, some students express disagreement and others ask for clarification. Throughout their explanation, it is clear that Marcie was eager to tell about her method. It is a lively discussion with Ms. Diaz listening and intervening to facilitate the interactions.

The class becomes an intellectual community

As described in the Professional Standards (NCTM, 1991), if students are to develop mathematical power, major changes in instruction are needed. Central to the shift envisioned by the Professional Standards authors, is negotiating social norms where classrooms become mathematical communities with all that is implied by that characterization. In mathematical communities, individuals assume responsibility for their actions and statements with reasoning and mathematical evidence as a test for viability rather than teachers acting as the mathematical authority (Cobb, Wood, Yackel, 1995). This call for change is broad based. In this book, classroom mathematics learning environments will be discussed. The central task of teaching is negotiating a classroom culture conducive to learning (Steffe, 1990).

Negotiating social norms. Students develop a set of expectations about each class they experience. These expectations are based on a set of social norms. The way each student acts in a class influences the microculture. A skillful teacher will negotiate rather than impose ways of interacting in the class. In some classrooms, students

29

expect to sit quietly, not talking except to answer questions posed by the teacher and then only when recognized. In such classes the structure imposed by the teacher dictates how students are to act and failure to comply with the rules results in disciplinary action. The norms in some classes might include joking around and distracting class activities. Such norms are obviously counter-productive.

By *social norms* we mean those ways of acting and interacting which are accepted by the group and that guide action. For example, when a student is explaining her mathematical reasoning to the group, it is the obligation of class members to attempt to make sense of what she says and to question what is not understood or accepted. Other social norms that might become part of the social fabric of a productive class are

1) students expect to be challenged and develop their solutions rather than following a set procedure demonstrated by the teacher,

2) students expect to construct their own methods and different students will carry out an operation in different ways,

3) students expect to collaborate with other students and serve as a community of validators, and

4) students expect the solution of a problem to take time and reflection.

In addition to the social norms listed above, it is important to negotiate sociomathematics norms (Yackel and Cobb, 1996). By *sociomathematics norms*, Yackel and Cobb refer to "what counts as a mathematics justification?" and "Why are some student explanations 'better' than others (we might say more elegant)?" Both of these sociomathematics norms are part of what it means to do mathematics.

Classroom cultures. While the teacher plays a role in constituting the learning environment, he or she does not establish it (Bauersfeld, 1996; Varela, Thompson, Rosch, 1993). Rather, a classroom culture is coconstructed by all the participants. The learners both contribute to and are strongly influenced by the culture of the classroom. The nature of each individual's participation in this construction is a subtle and complex activity. Just the presence of one person shapes the culture. The teacher may play an important role in negotiating an envisioned learning environment but the classroom culture that results is strongly influenced by the students. The reality of the classroom is dynamically developing and being interactively constituted (Bauersfeld, 1980).

In some classes, students enthusiastically participate in meaning making by questioning peers, developing their own methods, and justifying their explanations in the process of constructing their mathematics. In other classes, students see their role as following directions, carrying out procedures in prescribed ways and relying on the teacher as the source of knowledge. When instruction is skill based and rule governed, many students, in self-defense, adopt a "play the game called school" stance, attempting to decide what is required to get a good grade rather than forming the intention of making sense. The classroom culture is a major determiner of which stance students take. When the culture of the classroom encourages students to inquire, question, conjecture, collaborate and evaluate, students are more likely to learn mathematics than if they are required to listen to teacher explanations, complete practice exercises in a prescribed way and rely on the teacher to know if their answers are correct.

Bauersfeld (1996) contends that learning is in the interactions of individuals and thus gives importance to the culture of the classroom. For him, a culture where students are encouraged to construct meaning for themselves through interactions with others is central. If there are no student to student interactions, then the learning environment is impoverished. Thus establishing a learning environment where challenging others' mathematics reasoning is viewed as constructive and positive, translates into rich learning opportunities for students. Student-to-student interactions can play an important role in students becoming mathematically powerful.

Problem Centered Learning. One instructional model that has proved effective is problem centered learning (Wheatley, 1991). In problem centered learning, the class begins with a problem posed by the teacher, or perhaps by a student. The class is then organized into small groups (two or three students of similar capabilities) and the students work collectively in their groups on the tasks posed. After about 25 minutes, the students are assembled for class discussion in which students

Student-to-student communication fosters learning

31

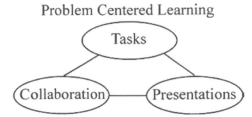

Problem Centered Learning

present to the class their solutions for consideration by the group which then serves as a community of validators. During the class discussion the teacher is nonjudgmental and the viability of solution methods is determined by the class, not the teacher. In problem centered learning the teacher has three main roles: selecting appropriate tasks based on her knowledge of the students, organizing the groups and listening carefully as they work and finally, facilitating the class discussions. The success of this model is dependent on the classroom culture and the social norms which have been negotiated.

Tasks. Students thrive on intellectual challenges. Many students who languish in a skills-based mathematics program come alive when given the opportunity to pursue nonroutine mathematics problems. Some of our most promising students turn away from mathematics because they see it as a set of procedures to be done in a prescribed way. Mathematics investigations should have the following characteristics:

- Be potentially meaningful to students
- Be problem based
- Be replete with patterns
- Encourage students to make decisions
- Lead somewhere mathematically
- Promote discussion and communication

Example:

Inspired by Kennedy's article in the Mathematics Teacher (Kennedy, 1993) the following week-long activity was designed. Annette Smith, a middle school teacher, used this activity with a seventh grade class. Students were provided with one inch dot paper and organized in groups to work on the following problem.

Draw all possible different triangles that have their corners on the dots. Develop a plan to find how many are there. How could you convince someone you have them all? [You may want to stop reading and try to draw all 29 possibilities]

Students were asked to draw triangles on the dot paper, cut them out and post them on the bulletin board. Examples of shapes posted are shown at the side. If students spotted duplicates, they were removed when agreement had been reached. In order to draw all possibilities, students had to develop a system for classifying the triangles. This generated

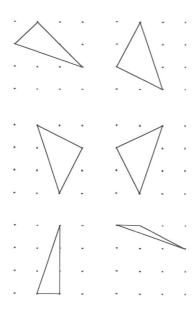

Portfolios are an effective way of assessing students

Pair students who can reciprocate

much discussion with a variety of classification plans used. The triangles on the bulletin board were often rearranged by the students to help develop patterns. Each day, Mrs. Smith would have a class discussion where students described their reasoning and conjectures. This generated much discussion. The classification of triangles by sides and angles was a topic of interest on several days. Students were surprised they could not draw an equilateral triangle on the four by four grid.

Extensions
- *What perimeters are possible? What is the largest perimeter? Smallest?*
- *What areas are possible? What is the largest area possible? Smallest?*
- *What angle measures are possible? What is the largest angle measure? Smallest?*

Assessment. Mrs. Smith had each student keep a portfolio of their investigations. They were also asked to write a description of their activity and what they learned. Students were encouraged to pose and investigate additional questions in this setting. Some students wondered how many triangles there would be if the grid was five by five. Others attempted to determine all quadrilaterals which can be formed on a four by four grid (There are many!).

This activity was potentially meaningful to all students - there was no technical language or special symbols that might be a block. The task seems simple, just draw triangles but proved to be quite challenging in that students had to develop a way of drawing the triangles systematically to know when all had been found. Students had to make many decisions and the activity promoted much discussion. The investigation was replete with patterns and involved fundamental mathematical ideas.

Collaboration. Cobb (1995) studied the interactions of second grade students working in pairs. Some of his findings are quite surprising. According to Cobb, if one of the students in a dyad becomes a mathematical authority, that is to say, the other student does not question the validity of what he or she does and defers to that person for decision making, little or no learning occurs. This finding conflicts with the folk wisdom of pairing a "good" student with a weaker person. The evidence is strong that pairs should be formed of students

33

who will challenge each other. It is the resolving of the perturbations resulting from disagreements that produces learning. Thus we should attempt to find pairings of individuals who will challenge each other's thinking in their attempt to give meaning to their mathematical experiences.

Class discussion. If students interpret the environment as a recitation, then the way they act will reflect that interpretation and they will see themselves in an evaluative position. In contrast, we can negotiate a classroom environment which is interpreted by students as a sense making place where their ideas are valued and listened to. When classrooms are seen as learning places rather than work places the dynamics can foster learning and risk taking.

The belief that a peer has something to say which is worth listening to must be fostered. But this fostering is a delicate matter. For example, if student utterances are filtered through the teacher, students do not develop a sense of communicating with one another. Repeating student comments "so all can hear" will discourage true discourse and the building of community.

Some students are "active" listeners in class discussions. They do not listen easily when sitting still and looking at the speaker but understand what is being said better when they are in motion. Some individuals think best while they are physically moving or doodling. Krutetskii (1976) reports that he gave a task to a five year old girl, she got up, did a somersault, sat back down and wrote the answer. While students moving around and perhaps making utterances can be distracting, we may want to explore ways of allowing certain students to be physically active during class discussion. Brad, a third grader was observed during class discussion to be playing with pencils and not looking at the speaker (Lo and Wheatley, 1994). Afterward, in a video recorded interview, he could describe what the speaker said, whether it made sense, what their intentions were, what other students where doing and how the teacher was reacting to the class. Brad could actually listen better when he was active. Some adults have the practice of doodling while listening to a speaker and claim they can attend more easily that way. Thus "Paying attention," that is, setting quietly with eyes on the

Students present their ideas for the class to consider.

34

teacher, is not a prerequisite for meaningful participation in class discussion.

Encouraging Creativity. It is vital that the teacher negotiate a set of social norms which foster curiosity, creativity and sense making. For example, beginning a class with a problematic task is one way of getting students involved in thinking mathematically. However, before discussing the value of such an approach, it is important to think about what is meant by a "problem." In order to design an appropriate task, the teacher must have some sense of what each student knows about the topic so that a task can be designed which is within their zone of potential constructions, i. e., it is challenging but possible. Further, the task should be problematic for the students. Once students have become engaged in a task, curiosity and creativity can be encouraged by extending the problem, by asking 'what if" questions and encouraging students to formulate related problems. As Brown and Walter (1983) point out, having students pose problems takes mathematics to a higher plane, a plane where they are acting mathematically in quite powerful ways.

Summary. The dynamic culture of a mathematics classroom has a strong influence on the nature of mathematics learning. As a teacher develops a vision of mathematics classrooms compatible with the recommendations of NCTM (1991), steps can be taken to negotiate a culture of the classroom that encourages intellectual autonomy, curiosity, and sense making. A classroom culture will develop and the teacher can play a vital role in negotiating, not legislating, a learning environment which encourages students to become mathematically powerful (Cobb, Yackel, Merkel, Wheatley, 1988).

The social norms which come to be established in a class will constrain or facilitate the mathematics learning of students. One model of instruction which has proven effective is problem centered learning (Nicholls, Cobb, Yackel, Wood, Wheatley, Trigatti, and Perlwitz, 1991; Wood and Sellers, 1996). Problem centered learning is designed to encourage students to construct knowledge for themselves in ways that the learning will be lasting. As students work collaboratively on challenging tasks and have their ideas tested in an intellectually community, they develop confidence

"What if" questions encourage creativity

Social norms are negotiated, not legislated

35

and knowledge. The explain-practice method of teaching has serious weaknesses and is proving to be ineffective if not debilitating. New technologies allow attention in mathematics classes to be focused on concepts rather than procedures, thus freeing students to consider more challenging and meaningful tasks.

As we learn more about classroom cultures and how they form, we are in a better position to design more effective learning environments which empower students. For too long schools have encouraged a transmission view of teaching. More recent theoretical and practical studies have shown that knowledge cannot be transmitted but that meaning is evoked by each individual's experiences in a learning setting. By encouraging students to construct mathematical patterns and relationships, we can help them become powerful learners for a lifetime.

Class Openers

Class openers can enhance the learning that occurs with the main activities. Students respond well to a change in their activity during a lesson. One way of providing variety in a lesson is to start the class with a five-minute attention-getter. Further, well designed lesson openers smooth the transition from one subject to another and help students focus on doing mathematics. Described below are activities that have proven effective as lesson openers.

Quick Draw

Quick Draw has proven to be a wonderful activity. It helps students focus on mathematics at the beginning of a lesson, stimulate thought and develop vocabulary. Kids love it. It is also an effective way of negotiating the social norms that facilitate mathematics learning.

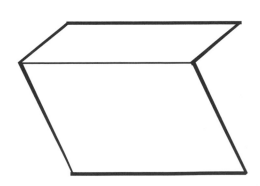

T: What did you see and how did you draw it?
(Teacher is communicating that the figure
may be seen in more than one way which
encourages intellectual autonomy.)
Sarah: I saw a folded sheet of paper.
T: Was it folded toward you or away from you?
(Teacher is showing a direct interest in the student's interpretation.)
Sarah: It was folded toward me.

Carlos:	I saw it the other way.
T:	What do you mean you saw it the other way?
Carlos:	The paper was folded back, not forward.
T:	I see what you mean. Did anyone see it another way?
Shanna:	I saw the top and front of a box.
T:	What do you mean? Where is the box?
Shanna:	See (as he goes to the screen and points) this is the top of the box and this is the front.
John:	Oh yeah, I see what he means!
Marsha:	It looks like the top and back of a box.
Ing-Gee:	I see two sorta diamond shapes.
T:	You mean these? They are called parallelograms. So you saw it as a flat figure? (Teacher uses technical mathematical language without criticizing the student.)
Ing-Gee:	Yes.
T:	How did you draw it?
Ing-Gee:	I drew the middle line first and then the two lines slanting up and then the top line. I drew the bottom part the same way.

Quick Draw is very effective in developing spatial sense and encouraging students to communicate their mathematical ideas. A collection of Quick Draw Shapes can be found in the book *Quick Draw: Developing Spatial Sense*, available from the publisher, <u>Mathematics Learning.</u>

Quick Build

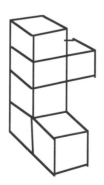

Using Snap Cubes or Multilinks, make a 3-D object such as the one shown here, hold it up for all to see and ask students to make the shape with their cubes. Continue holding up the cube as students work at their building. When you see that most students have completed their construction, ask them to compare it with others near them. Often you will find that some students have made the mirror image (left glove rather than right glove). This is a wonderful opportunity to help students think about 3-D symmetry. Continue with other shapes. You may want to have a student make a shape (specify the number of cubes) and take your role.

The next step is to present drawings of objects made with cubes on the overhead projector, show the figure for just two seconds and ask the students to make it with their cubes. Shown below are a few sample configurations you might use.

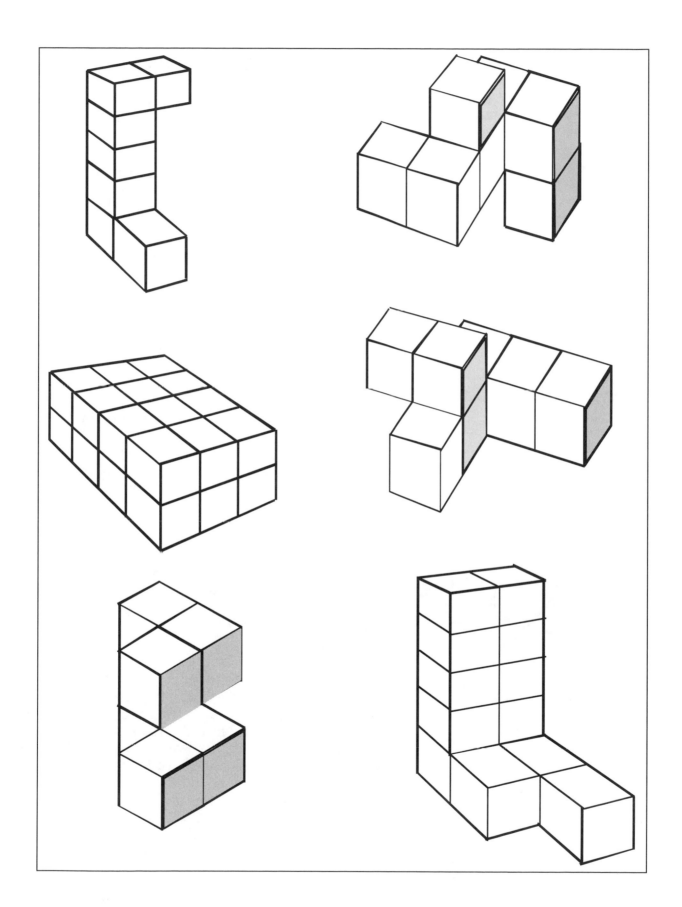

Spot the Dots

This classroom opener is designed to help students build mental images of numbers. It also serves as a basis for multiplication. Some teachers have found it valuable to use this activity frequently.

Procedure:

Without the students seeing, arrange a set of chips in a rectangular pattern on an overhead projector. Say "I will show you a set of objects for a short period of time. Try to form a mental picture so you can determine how many there are and how they are arranged. You will not have time to count them."

Show the arrangement for 2-3 seconds (no longer!). After students have had time to think about how many there are, show it again for 2-3 seconds. Then ask, "How many did you see?" As students respond ask the class how they saw the chips. Finally, uncover the chips and have students continue explaining how they saw the objects arranged. As you continue with this opener on subsequent days, increase the difficulty of the tasks by using more chips but keep to rectangular arrangements. Don't hesitate to use large numbers of chips such as a five by six array. Challenge your students.

Tangrams

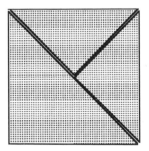

This is another activity that encourages students to develop their mental imagery. In this activity students use their set of Tangrams to make a shape they see briefly.

Procedure:

Use a transparency to flash a completed tangram puzzle like the one shown here on the overhead for THREE seconds. Students use their own set of Tangram pieces to recreate from memory what they saw. After about one minute, flash the overhead on for a second look. If necessary, turn on the overhead for a third time and leave it on while students complete and check their work. Initially, make outlines of the shapes you are going to project and give each student a sheet with this outline as they complete the activity. Later, you can have students recreate the shape they see projected without the help of an outline. You can also ask a student to be the teacher and make a shape for the class.

Mental Arithmetic

At the beginning of math time, write on the board several addition or subtraction tasks such as 37 + 23 or 40 − 14 and ask students to take a minute to do them mentally. Follow this by asking selected students to explain to the class how they did the problem. The discussion is very important so be sure to encourage students to listen carefully and explain fully. When one student has explained a method ask, "Did anyone do it another way?" Choose tasks that you judge to be challenging but possible for your class. As you continue with this mental arithmetic opener on subsequent days, increase the difficulty of the tasks by using larger numbers or using three or more addends. You will be surprised how your students become able to do quite complex computations mentally.

What's My Rule?

What's My Rule is one of the most powerful mathematics activities that can be used at any grade level. It is a whole class activity in which one person, initially the teacher, thinks of a rule such rule being used by seeing what the rule does to a number. For example if the rule is 'add five,' someone calls a number and the leader says the number given by the rule. If Sally thinks she knows the rule, she can say the word "rule!" and the process is reversed; the leader gives Sally a number and she reports the number she thinks the rule would give. Players are asked not to describe the rule so all may continue to be involved. This process continues until most students know the rule, at which time there is a discussion of the rule. At this point the teacher asks, "What do you think the rule is?" Students can describe the rule in the way they are thinking. Different but equivalent formulations of the rule may be expressed. For example if the rule is two times a number plus four, some might say, "Take two more than the number and double it."

Sample game:

T: I have a rule in mind. Someone give me a number.

P1: 4

T: 9

P2: 10

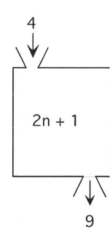

T: 21
P3: 5
T: 11
P4: Rule!
T: 8
P5: 17
T: Yes, that is what my rule gives.
P5: 0
T: 1
P2: Rule!
T: 20
P2: 31
T: No, that is not what my rule gives.
P6: Rule!
T: 6
P6: 13
T: Yes, that is what my rule gives.

Now let's talk about the rule. How were you thinking about it?

P2: I doubled the number and added one.

P7: I multiplied the number by two and added one.

Paper folding

In this activity, the teacher folds a piece of paper in half once or twice, cuts off parts and asks students to draw what it would look like when unfolded. While Quick Draw promotes the formation and re-presentation of images, Paper Folding provides opportunities for students to transform images. In drawing the shape of the paper by looking at the still folded paper, students can transform the image and "look at it in their mind." Many mathematics tasks are accomplished by imaging a transformation of a geometric shape or other mathematics symbolizations. For example, drawing a diagram can often be used to solve word problems. In order to draw the diagram, the individual must first form a mental image of the appropriate diagram and, many times, transform it.

Materials: Unlined paper for students and teacher, pencils, one pair of scissors.

Directions:

Distribute unlined paper to students and ask them to draw horizontal and vertical lines to partition it into four equivalent regions. This provides defined space for them to draw four different shapes. Using an 8 1/2 by 11 blank sheet of paper, fold it to form a 5 1/2 by 8 1/2 rectangle.

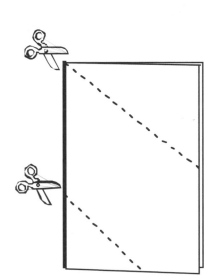

"I am folding this piece of paper. Notice that the fold is here (holding hand vertically on the left edge of the folded paper). Now watch. I will cut this folded paper." With students watching, make the cuts shown. "Now draw what this paper would look like when unfolded. Remember, the fold is on this side." Hold the folded paper, which has now been cut, high so all can see until students have had an opportunity to draw a shape on their paper. "I will now unfold the paper. Compare your drawing with this (holding the unfolded paper high for all to see)."

Now ask the class, "How did you draw the shape?"

Sample student responses:

Mike: I unfolded it in my mind.

Sue: I drew the shape I saw and then drew the reflection of it on this side. That gave me the solution.

This task requires little preparation or materials but pays big dividends. The initial cuts can be simple and progress to very challenging. Corners can be cut off, triangles, squares, or rectangles cut out of various edges. Students soon see that it makes a big difference whether the cuts are on the fold or a single edge. After students have had experience with single folds, the double fold presents a new challenge. In this case, the student must do two mental transformations, that is, unfolding twice.

A double fold

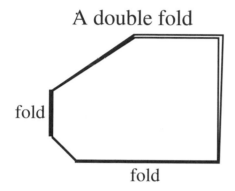

fold

fold

Paper Folding Examples

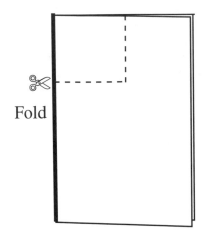

Fold

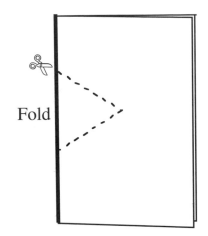

Fold

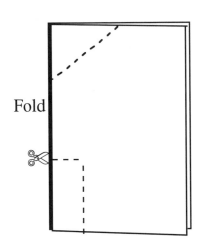

Fold

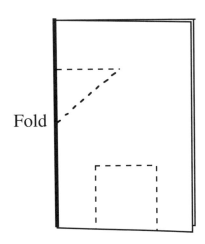

Fold

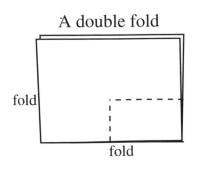

A double fold

fold

fold

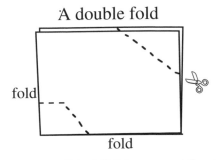

A double fold

fold

fold

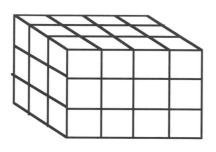

$7 + 5 =$
$6 + 1 + 5 =$
$6 + 6 = 12$

So $7 + 5 = 12$

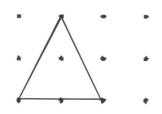

There is compelling evidence that imagery plays a significant role in mathematical reasoning. For example, a young child may add 7 + 5 by mentally "moving" 1 from the 7 to the 5 to form 6 + 6, a known double. Or a child might determine how many one inch cubes there are in a rectangular solid 3" by 3" by 4" by visualizing the solid as composed of three layers of 12. Whether working in a numerical or geometric setting, when students are engaged in meaningful mathematics rather than rote computation, it is quite likely they will be using some form of imagery. There is also evidence that imaging plays an essential role in many mathematicians' activity. Logic alone does not account for mathematical reasoning. It has been reported that mathematicians who feel they have a deep understanding have constructed some abstract image which makes the knowledge into a whole.

When doing mathematics, the nature of the images formed depends on prior mental constructions, intentions, and the situation under which the image is constructed. For example, a child might form an image of 'triangle' as having a horizontal base and a point above the base. If this image of a triangle is the child's only image of a triangle, then their concept of triangle is quite limited. A child has a richer concept of triangle when she or he can transform an image of a triangle flexibly. Tim, a third grader, was asked to draw all possible triangles on a 16 dot square grid. He drew the isosceles triangle shown and then hesitated for a long time. He then drew a triangle congruent to his first one but in another location. We discussed what it meant to be different. After more time he drew the next triangle shown. From these actions, it seemed that his image of a triangle was isosceles with a horizontal base. It was some time before he drew any other type of triangle.

What an individual constructs depends not only on their immediate experiences but also on their prior mental schemes. The line drawing shown was presented briefly to a class and they were then asked to draw what they saw (Quick Draw). During the discussion that followed, this figure was described as two squares, a small square

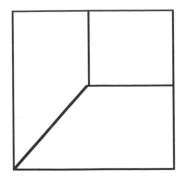

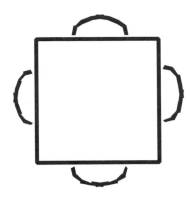

and two trapezoids, a hallway, a skylight, and a pyramid with the top cut off. Some individuals constructed an image of regions and others of joined segments. There were some two-dimensional and some three-dimensional interpretations. Even though the same figure was presented in the same manner to all individuals, the nature of the images formed varied greatly.

As an example of imaging in problem solving, consider the Long Table Problem:

Tiffany is arranging tables for a party. She has 15 square tables which she wants to put together to make one long table. Each of the small square tables seats one person on a side. How many people can be seated?

Most students successful in solving this problem elaborated their image of one table to twelve, some drawing out the twelve tables, and proceeding to count how many seats were available. One student made no marks on paper but explained he had a mental picture of the twelve tables in a row and he could "see" 12 seats on each side with one on each end. This student had powerful mental imagery. The individual differences in imaging among children are striking.

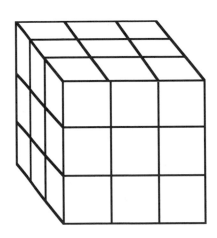

A fifth grade girl's solution to a mathematics problem shows the importance of imaging. The problem was "On a Rubik's Cube (3x3x3), how many small cubes have exactly two faces showing?" While at first she answered 24 (four on each of six faces), once she looked at a Rubik's Cube she quickly revised her answer and confidently said 12. In her second image, the cube was composed of layers and she could "see" how adjacent faces of the Rubik's Cube shared small cubes. Her first image of a cube as composed of six nonintersecting faces is a frequently reported image. The second is more sophisticated and, in this case, more useful in solving the question posed.

Meaningful mathematics learning is usually image-based. While there may be certain forms of mathematical reasoning which do not use imagery, most mathematical activity has a spatial component. If school mathematics is procedural, students may fail to develop their capacity to form necessary images of mathematical patterns and relationships. It is well documented that students who reason from dynamic images tend to be powerful mathematics students. When students are encouraged to develop mental images and use those images in mathematics, they show surprising growth. All students can learn to use images effectively. Thus, every mathematics teacher or parent should make improving spatial sense a priority.

In the primary grades, one of the most important tasks for the teacher is to provide opportunities for students to construct ten as an abstract unit (Cobb & Wheatley, 1988). In order to develop the number sense necessary for problem solving and the refinement of computation strategies, students must be able to think of ten as a unit (a whole) while at the same time think of it as ten ones (parts). Wheatley & Reynolds (1996) found that students' constructions of abstract units in number paralleled their construction of units in a geometric setting. For example, in constructing a repeating tiling pattern that could be extended indefinitely, the child must see a given shape as part of a larger whole, a part-whole relationship, just as in constructing ten as an abstract unit the child must see ten as composed of ten ones, while maintaining its "tenness."

In order to help her students construct ten as an abstract unit, one second grade teacher decided to use the following task with her students:

- How many trapezoids do you need to make a filled in triangle?
- What is the smallest triangle you can make?
- What is the largest?

Containers containing red Pattern Blocks (trapezoids) were provided. At the end of the first day's exploration students had decided that the smallest triangle possible was the one shown at the side. One student, Marta, had made the shape shown here using 12 trapezoids, which she presented to the class using overhead Pattern Block pieces.

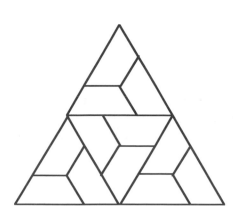

When asked how she knew there were 12 trapezoids in her triangle, she replied: "Well, I know there are four little triangles and each has three trapezoids, so there is three, six, nine, twelve." Immediately, other students began to notice that larger triangles they had made using trapezoids contained smaller triangles made from three trapezoids. This became an accepted way of exploring the different sized triangles students were making using the given trapezoid shape. Using cut outs of

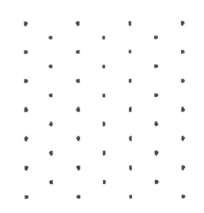

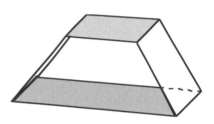

We see what we understand rather than understand what we see.

trapezoids and triangular dot paper they recorded the various triangles they made and described the patterns they developed to generate the triangles and "count" the number of trapezoids used.

A large trapezoidal shape was made using five sheets of poster board for the children to explore, using their whole bodies to climb in, out, and around, and push and pull into other shapes. Later, using 3 by 5 cards they made smaller trapezoidal shapes that they then combined to form triangles. On the last day they cleared a large space in the center of the room and combined the different triangle groups the students had made with the 3 by 5 cards into one large triangle and partitioned it into smaller triangles so they could determine the number of trapezoids they had used. Over the month they were focused and absorbed with the task and found it challenging.

At the end of this time, the teacher returned to number activity using balance tasks and word problems that involved double digit addition and subtraction. Immediately, it was evident that students had made great strides in their construction of ten as an abstract unit, even though they had not spent time in the previous month on these tasks. In the trapezoid task they had the opportunity to build abstract units in a geometric setting, an imaging activity that was now supporting their conceptualizing of ten as an abstract unit. The geometry activities involved using that part of their brain that forms and processes images and this utilization carried over to number activity.

Summary. In this section we have argued that the use of mental imagery can greatly enhance students' mathematics knowledge and reasoning. Too often, school mathematics tends to be procedural with little opportunity to use spatial sense. Such a curriculum may actually condition children's brains to think sequentially and mechanically which can be quite limiting. If on the other hand students are encouraged to use their spatial sense, their mathematics learning can be richer and more powerful. The activities in this book are designed to evoke images and encourage students to form and transform mental images in a number setting.

Problem Solving

When we trace problem solving in school mathematics, we find that problem solving has often been thought of as solving highly structured word problems appearing in texts. The "problem" is usually identified with the operation to be performed such as add, subtract, multiply, or divide. Often, the word problems were designed not so much to develop problem solving but to provide practice for prescribed computational procedures. A student can usually know what method to use by seeing the computational method illustrated in the preceding lesson. In many of today's textbooks, exercises designed to practice demonstrated methods are called problem solving.

The practice described in the preceding paragraph reflects a view of mathematics as facts and procedures. Seen in that light, the 'story problems' in textbooks serve that purpose. However, the prevailing view of mathematics today is quite different. As described in the National Council of Teachers of Mathematics Curriculum and Evaluation Standards, mathematics is the activity of constructing patterns and relationships. Thus, much of cognition is problem solving while little of what typically occurs in school classrooms could be considered problem solving because the learner is rarely allowed to make decisions; a specific method is required to be used.

Problem solving is what you do when you don't know what to do. If a student knows how to do the task then it is not problem solving. This underscores the fact that what is a problem for one person may not be a problem for another. We can suggest tasks but whether students take them as problems is an individual matter. Consider the following task.

Problem solving is what you do when you don't know what to do.

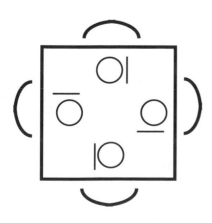

Tiffany is arranging tables for a party. She has 12 square tables which she wants to put together to make one long table. Each of the small square tables seats one person on a side. How many people can be seated?

This task has proven to be problematic for most primary school students. The ways students go about solving this problem are interesting. Some students will draw a picture of the tables and use a

49

variety of ways such as counting dots in arriving at a satisfactory answer. Marta made dots on her drawing for the people and counted-by-ones to arrive at a solution. Caleb reasoned that there would be 12 on each side and two at the ends and arrived at his answer by adding 12 + 12 + 2. This task cannot be solved by simply deciding this is an "add" or "multiply" problem and proceeding to carry out a computational procedure on two numbers.

What is problem solving?

The term problem solving has many meanings. Some textbooks use a four-step method to teach problem solving; understand the problem, formulate a plan, carry out the plan and check the solution. But problem solving is rarely so straight forward. Usually there is much cycling back; one may not really understand the problem until he or she has tried several approaches. Further, devising a plan may require considerable exploration such as trying a few numbers or drawing pictures.

Our study of individuals engaged in problem solving suggests that effective problem solving is much less organized than the Polya four steps would suggest (Trowell and Wheatley, 1994; Wheatley and Wheatley, 1982). Thus many of the tasks often used in mathematics classrooms as "problems" are in actuality exercises. It can be argued that as teachers we can only suggest tasks - individuals make their own problem to be solved. What is a problem for one person may be a trivial routine exercise for another. As Hundeide (1986) states "We tend to overlook the fact that problems only exist in relation to a background of expectations that are usually taken for granted" (p. 310). A student is engaged in problem solving when she experiences a situation that causes a perturbation - when the situation is unclear and no known methods seem to apply.

Polya's first step, understanding, is rarely accomplished before a plan is devised. Few scientists would state that they understand a problem before a solution has been obtained. In problem solving there is usually interpretation followed by a period of exploration in which patterns and relationships are constructed and mental images formed. Often, obtaining a solution to a stated question reveals fresh nuances which may suggest that the problem was not initially well understood.

Sfard (1994) provides convincing evidence that mathematicians do not feel they understand a problem until they have a wholistic image of the relationships. In her interviews, the mathematicians described carrying out procedures and solving problems and not understanding until much later, if at all.

Personal heuristics are constructed by the individual as she reflects on her experience, not as the result of direct instruction and practice. What to a university instructor may be an exercise can be a problem for students. On the other hand, "exercises" are not ruled out as problems – it depends on the student's knowledge and expectations. We have interviewed students for whom 83 - 38 was a problem. That is, they had constructed no procedure for determining an answer and thus had to problem solve to complete the task. The definition of problem solving used in this book does not exclude any task as being a problem for a student. Furthermore, we do not have in mind as problems just puzzle-type tasks or any specially contrived task such as the Tower of Hanoi. In contrast, much of what passes as problem solving in school mathematics is using a taught procedure on a similar word problem.

In problem solving, "understanding" develops throughout the problem solving process. Since we are social beings, any personal formulation of a problem is clearly a function of our interaction with others. The very act of asking questions reflects a stance, an orientation toward life. In the broadest sense, we cannot *give* students problems.

Problem solving instruction in schools is often the solving of well-defined questions based on certain information provided, frequently with the method specified. In reality, we can only suggest tasks - students make the problem they solve. For some, the "problem" might be writing something on their paper to get partial credit or to avoid looking stupid. Other students may interpret the "task" differently and choose to solve *their* problem, while others will make a problem from the task and become totally engrossed in making sense of the situation, not just obtaining an answer. They may even solve their problem in more than one way in order to verify their solution or pose new 'what if' questions, which they then explore and solve. Thus we cannot isolate problem solving from the broader context of knowing.

Ambiguous tasks may be more effective in promoting learning than well-defined questions. For example, consider the question, "How much paper will be required to wrap five identical cubes as a single present with no overlaps?" A few moments considering this situation will reveal that there are a variety of interpretations of this task. How are the blocks to be arranged? Will the paper be pulled taut or adhere to the sides of cubes? What is meant by "how much paper", area? Size of sheet? As students explore this task over several class periods presenting their interpretations, problems, solutions, and answers, significant learning opportunities are created. There are significant learning opportunities just in the act of interpreting the problem. As individuals in a social setting attempt to negotiate their interpretations of a problem, much can be learned by all students.

Heuristics

Problem solving heuristics are ways of coming to know a problem - actions that have the potential to lead to problem resolution. Heuristics differ from rules in that there is no guarantee that a particular heuristic will lead to an "answer." There is the danger that attempting to teach specific heuristics directly will result in the heuristics being viewed as rules. Three types of heuristics can be described; exploratory, general, and domain specific. Since heuristics are personal, it is possible that what is a general heuristic for one person may be domain specific for another. Yet it may be helpful to think in terms of the three categories posed.

Exploratory heuristics

If a task is taken as a problem by an individual, he or she may have no idea how to begin. The most fundamental of all heuristics is DO SOMETHING. What one actually does will depend on many factors including previously constructed schemes, intentions, and prior experiences with related problems. Doing something may involve mentally visualizing relationships, making a sketch, trying a number, testing a possible solution, using a special case, or any of a variety of other moves. Constructing units often proves helpful. Many students are not confident problem solvers because they believe good problem solvers know what to do and will write down the solution in an orderly set of steps. Since they don't know what "the first step" is, they do nothing. Once they come to believe there is no one first step and that problem solving involves exploration, they are on their way to becoming effective problem solvers.

General heuristics

Much attention has been focused on general problem solving heuristics (Mason and Burton, 1991; Polya, 1962; Wheatley and Wheatley, 1982). Most school mathematics textbooks list a set of problem solving heuristics to be taught. While there are differing views on how heuristics should be "taught," some researchers and many teachers have reported enhanced problem solving as a result of attention to heuristics. Lists of general heuristics usually include:

Draw a diagram,
Make a list or chart,
Look for a pattern,
Guess and test,
Try a simpler case, and
Work backwards.

There is little doubt that knowledge of options in problem solving is useful. The more a person is consciously aware of possible directions to take, the better he is able to deal with the uncertainty of problem solving. However, it does not follow that these heuristics should be the focus of instruction *prior* to the assignment of tasks. It is likely that heuristics will become part of a student's integrated knowledge if they evolve out of problem solving activity rather than being "taught" directly. As students engage in problem solving cooperatively and present their solution methods to the class, opportunities exist for the teacher to call attention and even name particular heuristics being used by the students. Thus Look-for-a-Pattern becomes the name for "What Marta was doing" rather than a method specified by the teacher to be used on a particular set of exercises.

Domain Specific Heuristics

Certain heuristics are domain specific. For example, in solving a geometry problem, it may be necessary to draw a diagram. Some domains of inquiry naturally suggest certain heuristics that are not useful in other settings. Each domain of knowledge may have heuristics that work well because of the type and nature of the knowledge organization.

Problem solving in mathematics involves abstract and varied tasks requiring the construction of high level abstractions and thus different cognitive mechanism may be operating. It is important for teachers to do a careful analysis of tasks and determine the essential constructions students need to make and then formulate tasks which provide potential opportunities for those constructions to be made.

In large part because of the particular philosophy of mathematics, attention has been focused on problem solving rather than problem posing. Problem solving has been framed as a machine-like activity performed by 'subjects.' But all cognitive activity is carried out by a person who has goals, intentions, expectations, and unique personal experiences. To ignore the individual in problem solving is to dehumanize teaching.

Personal heuristics

Wheatley and Wheatley (1982) report on the problem solving activity of grade six pupils. In their study, students were observed as they engaged in solving nonroutine problems. While students had an opportunity to learn six particular heuristics, wide individual differences were noted in the strategy use of students. Interviews were conducted with 102 students as they attempted five nonroutine problems. Not only were there heuristic preferences but particular heuristics tended to be favored on each of the problems. The strategies observed being used most often were, guess and test, make a list, look for a pattern, draw a diagram, simplify, and write an equation. When all five interview problems were considered, the order of heuristic use was guess and test, make a list, look for a pattern, and draw a diagram. Students showed definite strategy preferences. This study suggests that individuals solve problems in idiosyncratic ways; each person constructs methods that guide and influence his or her problem solving activity.

There is an innate drive in all of us to make sense of our experiences. We do not say make sense of our environment because some might interpret that to mean the environment is the same for all of us. Thus the young child thrives and learns by giving meaning to an experience and then testing the viability of that construction. In a similar way, if one evening you hear a noise as you are sitting in your living room, you try to give it meaning, to interpret it. This is problem solving. As we consider classroom situations and consider problem solving as a goal, we suspect the problem solving is not unlike learning as described above - it may be a difference in degree rather than kind. Too often, well-defined tasks are presented and the teacher expects a particular "answer." Few learning opportunities arise in such situations. However, if we encourage students to define their own problems, learning may occur. Or more importantly, an individual may experience a perturbation, which leads to a problem being formulated and perhaps solved.

Concepts make sense only if we have some abstract schema to organize and give meaning to the concept to be learned (Egan, 1988). The teacher may have a clear understanding of a particular concept but her explanation may not be intelligible to students who have not constructed the prerequisite schemas. This has been called the learning paradox (Cobb, Wood, Yackel, 1992). Even the use of concrete materials cannot always help students give meaning to the concepts. While attempting to explain concepts is unlikely to be effective, teaching through problem solving has rich potential. As we plan educational experiences for students, problem solving in the broader sense provides a basis for meaning making. Sensory experiences may prove invaluable as the individual is engaged in giving meaning to a problem he or she has posed but to act as though students learn simply from the "concrete" to the abstract may not be useful.

While attention to problem solving heuristics may be helpful, training students to use particular strategies such as draw a diagram or work backwards may not be. Students profit from constructing their own methods and then explaining their solution methods to the class (Lo, Wheatley, Smith, 1994; Wheatley, 1991). The teacher may wish to assist students in becoming more aware of the strategies they are using and even attaching names to their methods. Explaining and justifying solution methods is part of an instructional strategy called Problem Centered Learning which is ideal for problem solving instruction (Wheatley, 1991).

Exploration

Perhaps the most important characteristic of successful problem solvers is an exploratory mind set. Helping students overcome a rule orientation should be a major goal of teachers. Until students can adopt an exploratory stance they are unlikely to become effective problem solvers. Successful problem solvers approach a "problem" in a relaxed manner realizing they have a repertoire of things to try. Some persons actually enjoy the challenge of the unknown while other persons become anxious when they don't immediately see how to solve the problem. Good problem solvers suspend judgment and realize they are likely to try several approaches in coming to know the problem.

Wheatley and Wheatley (1982) concluded that adopting an exploratory mind-set was the most important factor in successful problem solving. "Children seem to learn a rule-oriented mindset in school that inhibits problem solving performance" (p. 116). It was those students who shifted away from a rule orientation and explored problems who were the successful problem solvers. In the Wheatley and Wheatley study, a group of students who continued to study a textbook driven curriculum performed poorly on a five-item problem solving test. In fact, the lower third of the treatment groups out performed the highest third of the control group! The following task was used with the 102 students interviewed.

I am thinking of two numbers. The sum of the numbers is 33 and their difference is 15. What are the two numbers?

Students in the control group would typically compute 33-15 and write down an answer. Students who had studied problem solving for 18 weeks would often perform the same computation but with no expectation that it would yield an answer; they were just exploring the problem. They followed this exploratory move by other computations in a guess and test mode. This problem proved challenging for all groups but none of the 34 students in the control group solved the problem correctly. For those students who were successful, an exploratory stance was evident.

Problem solving viewed as learning

In this book a particular view of learning is taken, one that seems especially appropriate for school mathematics in the nineties. Moving away from the logical positivist perspective which has dominated the sciences in this century (Kuhn, 1970), mathematics can be thought of as the construction of patterns and relationships - it is a personal activity. Adopting a Piagetian perspective, learning results from the neutralizing of perturbations and thus necessarily results in some reorganization, or elaboration of existing schemes (Steffe, 1993). Problem solving can be thought of as reducing the healthy tension resulting from a perturbation.

We must recognize that all problem solving occurs in a culture, in a social organization. While the constructivist perspective focuses on individual cognition, there is acknowledgment that problem solving is heavily influenced by social interactions. Actually, these interactions can support the development of powerful heuristics by each individual. As students collaborate to make sense of and solve problematic tasks and then share their person solutions with the class, there is an opportunity for students to hear how others approached the problem. In a problem centered classroom it is not uncommon to hear remarks such as, "Oh, I like the way Stephanie thought of that! I'm going to try that next time."

Problem solving is a comprehensive activity which is influenced by intentions, the setting (Brown, Collins and Duguid, 1989; Lave, 1988), our interactions with others, the personal schemes we have constructed, as well as the tasks set by an instructor. It must be recognized that while the schemes are described as personal, this does not imply they are constructed independent of social interactions. We are social beings and a major source of experience and perturbation is our community of others (Cobb and Bauersfeld, 1995).

Summary

Each person builds a personal set of problem solving heuristics even if specific heuristics have been experienced in the classroom setting. But central to success in problem solving is an exploratory mind-set; students who fail to break out of a school induced rule/formula orientation have little success as problem solvers. Richards (1991) argues for abstract tasks - tasks which are potentially meaningful. He asserts that mathematics is inherently abstract - that students can and should be involved in abstractions. He questions the assumption that students are only motivated by what they think will be useful to them. Students can and should come to value activities which are abstract in nature (Egan, 1988). As we plan educational experiences for students, problem solving in the broader sense provides a basis for meaning making. As Prawat (1993) says, "Creating a sense of wonder and awe in students should be our highest priority. I am concerned that the current preoccupation with *practical* problem solving does not advance us very far toward achieving that goal" (p. 14).

Because we live in a fast changing society, the ability to cope with novelty, to deal successfully with nonroutine problems is important. In another sense, becoming a problem solver may enhance the quality of life - it may lead to esthetic pleasure and even enhance the quality of someone else's life. Becoming knowledgeable may be the most important thing persons can do for themselves and society. There are many situations in which a knowledge of science and mathematics may be useful. The question is how we come to know. Problem solving is a primary way of knowing.

Multiplicative Reasoning

Multiplication is not the child of addition

array

Multiplication is usually taught as repeated addition; the number sentence 4 X 5 = 20 is usually explained as four groups of five. While this approach does prove useful at times, it is quite limiting. Considering multiplication as an operation in its own right has much merit. A case can be made for thinking of multiplication fundamentally as an array, that is, four dots across and five down. Thus 4 X 5 might evoke the image of a four by five arrangement of dots. We could, of course choose to think of the array as four rows of five. In making sense of an array, it can be partitioned in many ways to decide how many in all. For example, some children will see a 4X5 array as a four by four with another row of four. The repeated addition interpretation can follow from the array approach while it is unlikely that students will learn to think multiplicatively if repeated addition is their primary multiplication model. The concept of multiplication requires coordinating the elements in the rows with the elements in the columns.

Recent studies that we have conducted suggest that the array approach provides a good foundation for developing multiplicative reasoning. We have presented students with a photograph measuring three inches across and five inches high and asked them what the height would be if the photograph was enlarged so that the new image is 12 across. A majority of middle school students give 14 as their answer, reasoning additively that five is two more than three so 14 is the number which is two more than twelve. These responses provide strong evidence that many students are not learning to reason multiplicatively under the conventional approach. Thinking in arrays can help solve this problem.

A grade four child was asked: "What is eight times three?" and answered:

Three, six, nine, twelve, thirteen, fourteen, fifteen, sixteen, seventeen, eighteen, nineteen, twenty, twenty-one, twenty-two, twenty-three, twenty-four. . . Twenty-four.

While this person obtained the correct answer of 24, there was little evidence of multiplicative reasoning in her activity. In this case, she obviously took 8 x 3 as a trigger to count-on. Certainly, the act of counting-on by three requires concentration but it is not an indication she is using a multiplicative scheme - she counts to get an answer. The fact that she decided to count-on suggests she has given some meaning to the question - but not necessarily <u>multiplicative</u> meaning. Similarly, when a student responds "Twenty-four" and says, "I just knew it" she is not <u>exhibiting</u> any knowledge of multiplication. She may have been 'drilled' on her multiplication facts, which have little meaning for her.

Just as we can conclude that a child is thinking additively when she determines 5 + 7 by saying, "Six plus six is twelve; five is one less and seven is one more. . . twelve" a child could be said to be thinking multiplicatively when she, for example, says: "Six times seven is forty-two because six times six is thirty-six and six more is forty-two." In this case there is evidence of using units of six as an object. In the example above the child is able to decompose the 7 of 6 x 7 into 6 + 1 and use the result meaningfully. Further, the 6 and 1 refer to sixes, not ones. There is two-dimensionalness in this activity - a coordination of units of units of units. As another example, a child who determined the number of cookies when 36 cookies are shared fairly among 3 persons by saying "If each person had ten that would be 30. There are two more threes in the six left over, so the answer is 12." is thinking multiplicatively - again a decomposition. Both examples can be imaged using an array structure

Students in a fifth grade class were finding the number of cubes in a three dimensional array of cubes, e.g., a two by three by four block. Paula, who had used A = l x w x h to arrive at 24 said, "But the corner cube gets counted once when you find the length, once for width, and once for height. So you can't get the number of cubes by multiplying the three numbers." She was perplexed by the apparent contradiction as she attempted to form disjoint sets. This is a student who was functioning at the top level (for this class) but was perplexed about the formula. The issue is "What is multiplication?" To conceptualize multiplication is to construct an array structure and to realize that each element in a n by m array is simultaneously in a row and column.

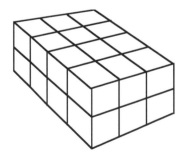

This is a sophisticated construction that requires a high level of abstraction. It is difficult, in part, because one has to go beyond disjoint sets. How many students make this construction? How many students experience activities that encourage this construction?

The problem below may help students think multiplicatively.

Kim made a game board of five rows of squares with six squares in each row. Later, Kim decided she wanted the game board to have one more row with one more square in each row. How many MORE squares would this new game board have?

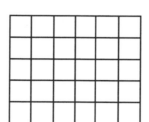 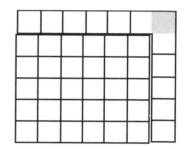

In this problem, a student is confronted with determining the number of squares when there is one more row and one more column. The answer is obviously **not** obtained by adding five and six. A solution to this problem involves the coordination of rows and columns - a multiplicative act. The child must consider the overlap of the new row with the new column which have a square in common.

We have found that showing arrays of dots briefly on the overhead and asking students "How many did you see?" is a good way to help students get beyond addition and begin thinking multiplicatively. For example, the array of dots shown at the side would be exposed briefly and shown again if necessary. Then students are asked "How many dots did you see and how were they arranged?". The discussion is an integral part of this activity. As students try to make sense of the ways others experience the arrangement of dots they are challenged to coordinate units. Seeing three groups of five is not the same as seeing five groups of three. They are however complementary views and require students to think of a particular dot as being part of a group of five and a group of three – a coordination of nondisjoint units. A selection of arrays for use as overhead transparencies to be used in this way are shown on following pages. Multiplication is about units of units of units. The task below illustrates units thinking.

> Suppose we have 24 books arranged in eight groups of three. How many more groups of three are needed to have 36?

In this task, there are singleton units, units of three and a unit of 24. A student might first determine that 12 more books are needed and then find how many units of three there are in 12.

Traditionally, the elementary mathematics curriculum has focused on addition and subtraction in the primary grades and multiplication and division in the later years. Such a separation of mathematical ideas may seem attractive to us as adults; it appears as a logical sequence that leaves the "more difficult" mathematics till later. However, from the learner's perspective, such sequencing has been found to be debilitating (Murray, Olivier, & Human, 1998). Students become so entrenched in their counting and additive thinking approaches that many do not develop the multiplicative thinking necessary to succeed in middle and high school mathematics.

It is possible, and advisable, to provide tasks in the primary grades which have the potential to focus the students' thinking on multiplicative relationships. Activities that provide opportunities for students to begin thinking multiplicatively include:

> Quick dot
> Balances
> Non-routine problem solving

In the Quick Dot activities, arrangements that invite students to construct arrays are useful for developing multiplicative thinking. For example

Sally: I saw four on top [row], and another four [lower left], and another four [lower right]. So there are three fours.

Morgan: I saw four rows with three dots in each.

David: There are two six's, six on the left and six on the right.

Tan: There's two three's to make six, and another two to make the other six.

Sally and Morgan's ways of describing the arrangement are complementary. This provided an opportunity for the teacher to ask the class:

"How are these ways different?"
"Are they the same in any way?"
David drew on his experiences with the various card and domino games to separate the dots into two groups of six dots, a pattern he recognized as a collection of six. Tan recognized columns of three dots in the collections of six dots that David described. This is also related to Morgan's way of seeing four "rows of three" dots. Each of these ways of "seeing" the dots provided an opportunity for students to begin thinking in arrays, which we have found supports their development of multiplicative thinking.

Another setting for developing these ideas is the balance format discussed earlier. In the balance tasks, it is possible to use an example like shown at the side to build multiplicative reasoning. Initially students may simply see this as "repeated addition." However, as students refine their methods for solving these tasks they begin to discuss their ideas in ways that can support their development of multiplicative thinking.

A collection of nonroutine problems that can be used to help develop multiplicative thinking is provided in Appendix A.

Part II

Pupil Activities

Dot Patterns

The Dot Pattern activity is designed to encourage students to think of objects as collections rather than things to be counted. By showing a set of dots briefly and asking how many did you see, counting is discouraged. Students need to build mental images associated with numerals and spoken number words. Too many students come to rely on counting to determine sums and differences rather than developing thinking strategies such as doubles plus one for 6 + 7. Counting is the only way many middle school students can determine 8 + 5. Unless students learn to think in collections they will be limited in their mathematical growth.

Prepare overhead transparencies from the dot patterns provided in this section. Choose the number of dots to challenge but not overwhelm your students. Show a pattern of dots for two or three seconds and ask, "How many did you see?" Show the dots again but avoid showwning them for more than three seconds. Students are conditioned to processing visual images quickly from watching TV commercials. After this second look, ask, "How many did you see and how were they arranged?" Encourage many students to explain how they saw the dot patterns. This discussion is important. As you continue to use this activity on a daily basis, increase the number of dots shown. You may want to vary the activity by using transparent plastic chips or coins to prepare a dot pattern on the overhead. Keep challenging students with more and more dots. The goal is that students will develop mental images associated with numbers and then be able to use these images in doing mathematics.

As a related activity, have students show, say six on their fingers. If students put up fingers one at a time, encourage them to show it all at once. Every student should have a finger pattern that can be shown immediately. For example if you ask students to show seven, they should be able to immediately show five on one hand and two on the other. Putting up fingers one at a time is unacceptable - we want them to develop finger patterns and not have to 'make' the number each time.

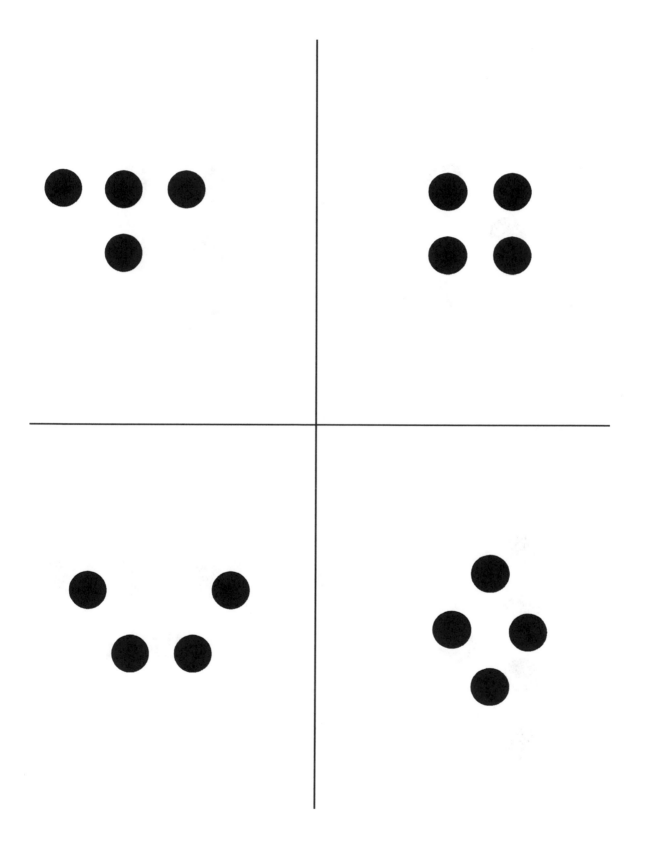

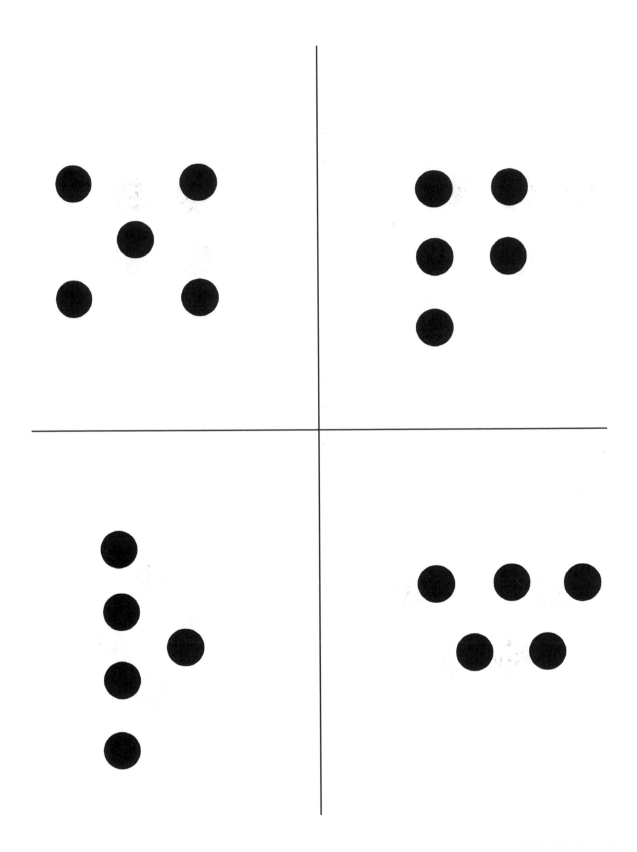

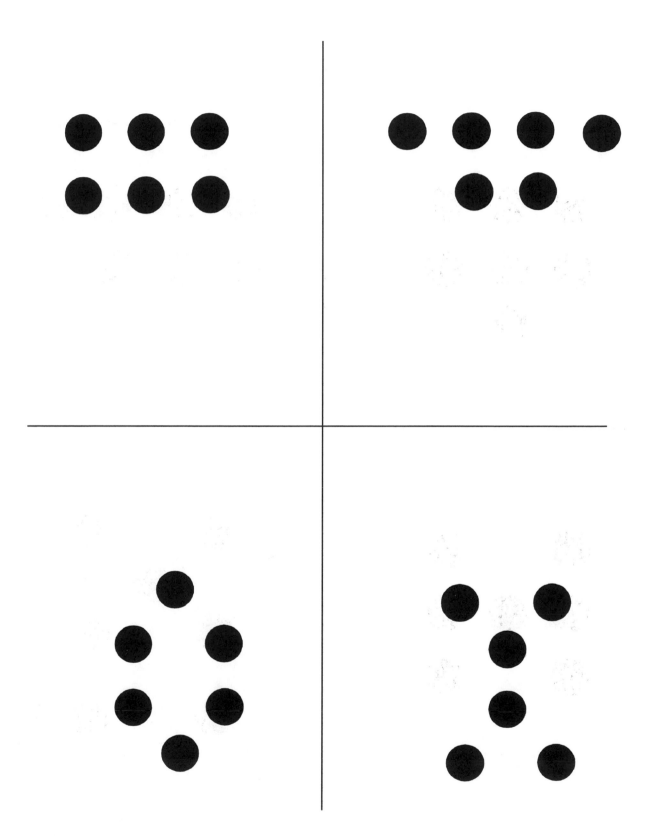

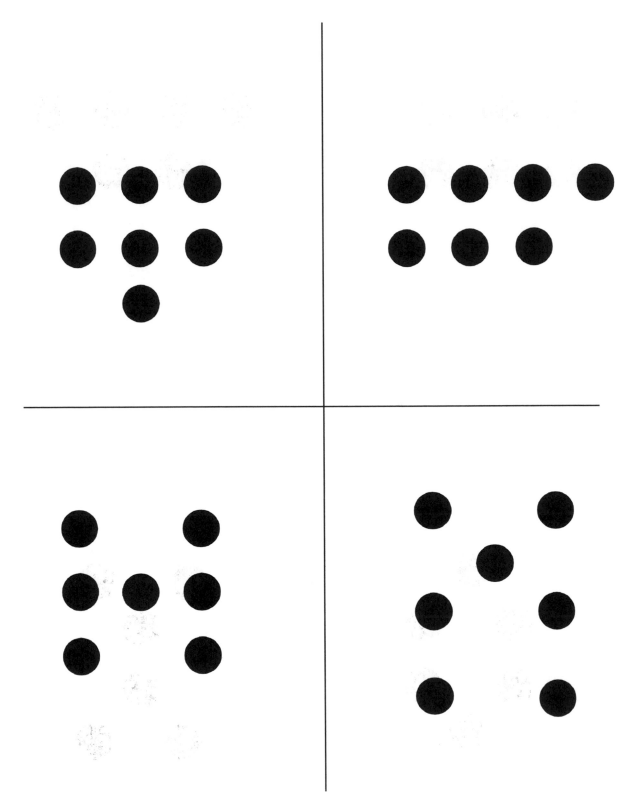

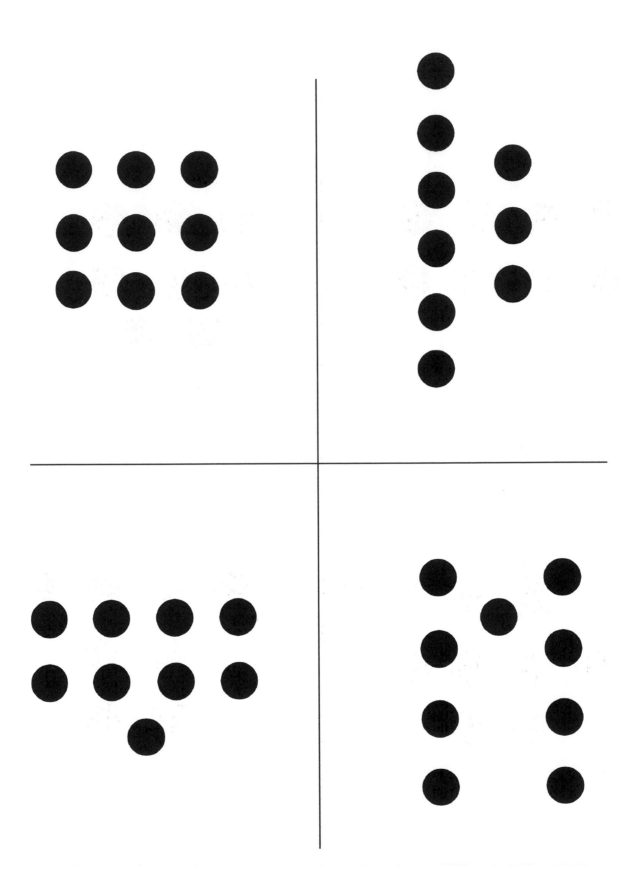

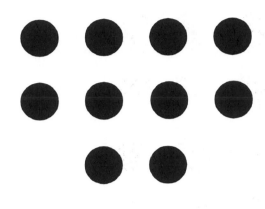

Ten Frames

Counting often becomes a routine that students perform without thinking. Mathematics is a cognitive activity and such rote actions as counting can lead students to act mechanistically which is not engaging and certainly not mathematical. An over reliance on counting can be quite debilitating. One of the themes of this book is that students become strong mathematically through the use of imaging. Kindergarten and first grade students can come to determine the numerosity of a set without counting and this leads to mathematical power. The emphasis can be on the collection rather than just the number word sequence.

Determining the number in a set without counting is an important step in a child's mathematics development. A dependence on counting can mitigate against sense making which should always be a goal of mathematical activity. While counting-by-ones may be appropriate at times, it can become a method students depend on to add and subtract long after they are capable of using number patterns.

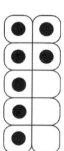

Ten Frames encourage students to form mental images that they can use in determining the number in a set without counting: it fosters the development of thinking strategies. As students mentally "move" dots to form familiar patterns, they are developing flexibility of thought and dynamic imagery. Transforming images to solve problems is at the heart of doing mathematics. Students may see three blank spaces in one Ten Frame and move three from another Ten Frame to make a ten. This "making ten" is most powerful and leads to efficient ways of adding and subtracting.

Ten Frames provide a setting for students to develop thinking strategies. Thinking strategies such as compensation (7 + 9 is 16 because 8 + 8 is 16) or going-through-ten (7 + 6 = 13 because 7 and 3 more make ten with three left over) are among the most useful ways of thinking about number we know.

Ten Frames have two aspects, the number of spaces (10) and the number of dots. The use of ten frames encourages the coordination of these two numbers with ten as a frame of reference. By using Ten Frames, students come to relate each number to ten and to its complement with ten. When a student sees a ten frame with seven dots, she has the opportunity to relate seven to ten and relate the complement, three, to both seven and ten.

Five Frames

Although constructing ten as a mathematical object is an important goal in elementary school mathematics, ten is a large number for one to make all at once - few persons can look at a set of dots and know there are exactly ten. For this reason Five Frames are recommended to be used prior to Ten Frames.

Because we have five fingers, five can become a landmark number for young children as they construct numbers for themselves. Five objects is also within young children's ability to quickly look at and know how many without counting. In this way, five can become a building block for six (one more than five) and seven (two more than five). Subsequently, ten can be thought of as two fives. Using Five Frames encourages students to construct an image of five as a reference. Showing a Five Frame with three dots provides students opportunities to think of three as a collection and relate it to two, the number of unfilled spaces, and to five. In this way, three can have a richer meaning than just the word we say after "two" and before "four."

Ten Frame activities

On an overhead projector, show a single Ten Frame with some but not all of the spaces filled. Show it for about three seconds (no longer!). Provide a second look. Ask students, "How many dots did you see?" "How did you see them?" This activity should be used for short intervals of ten minutes each day until students are able to determine the numbers easily. Then move to double Ten Frames. As students are able to readily determine the number and explain how they determined their answer, increase the number of dots used. Encourage students to explain how they saw the dots arranged. The discussion of the different ways students "see" the dots arranged is an essential component of this

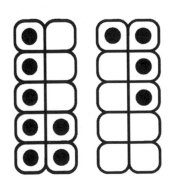

activity. Note that using double Ten Frames, students are actually adding without having the prompts provided by abstract symbols that may not evoke meaning. Students come to realize they can make sense of mathematics in their own way and not have to rely on remembering some method they were shown. Intellectual autonomy is promoted.

Occasionally, on completion of the Ten Frame activity, you might ask them to choose one of the ten frame examples just completed, draw it, and write about how they saw the arrangement. These can be left on display on the bulletin board for a few days so students can have another opportunity to think about the different strategies others are using. Later, these can be placed in student journals or portfolios as evidence of their number development.

A blank form of each type is included so that you may easily prepare additional Frame activities.

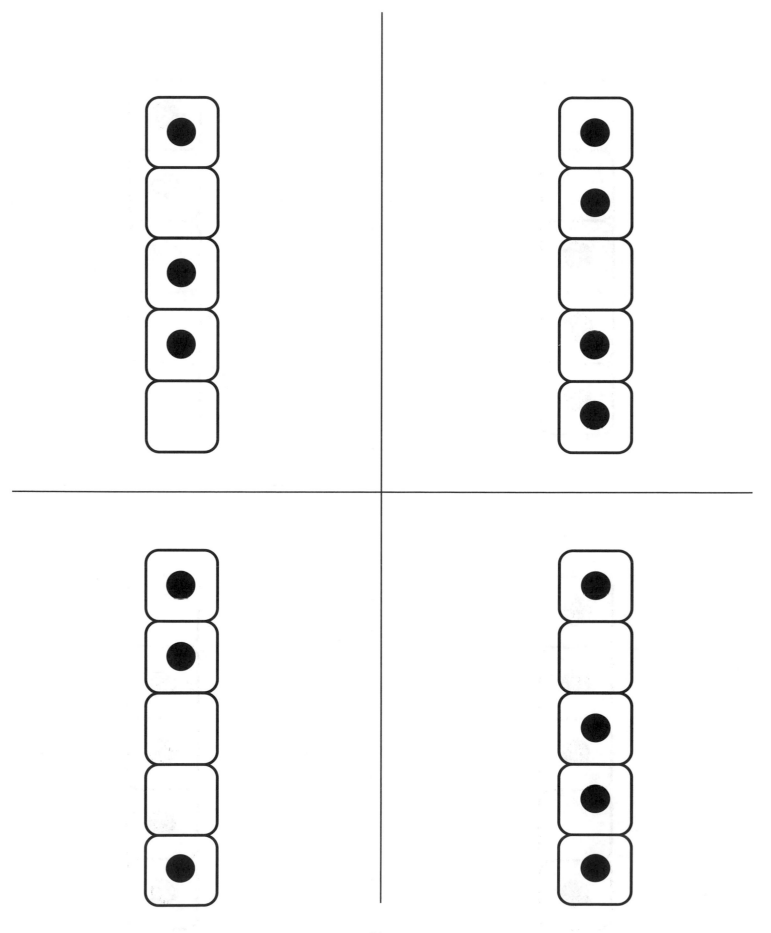

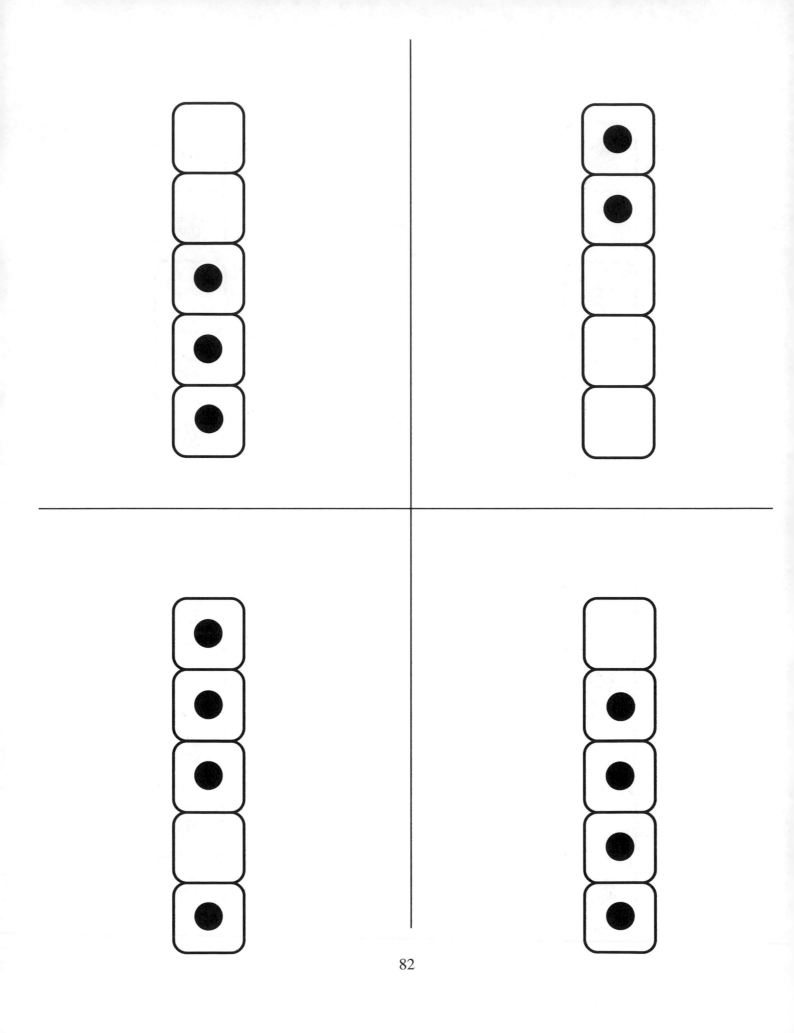

82

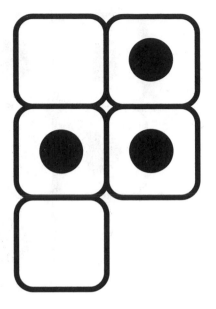

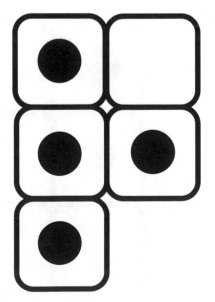

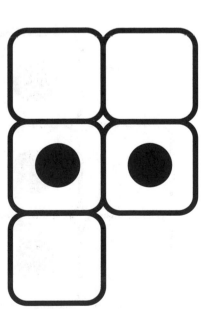

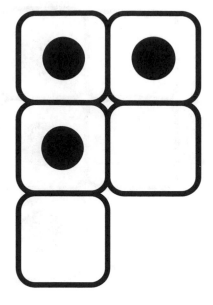

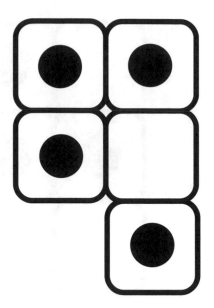

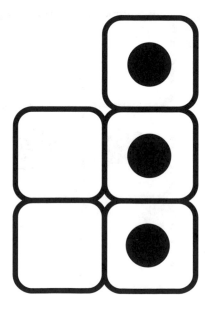

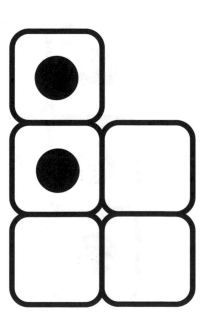

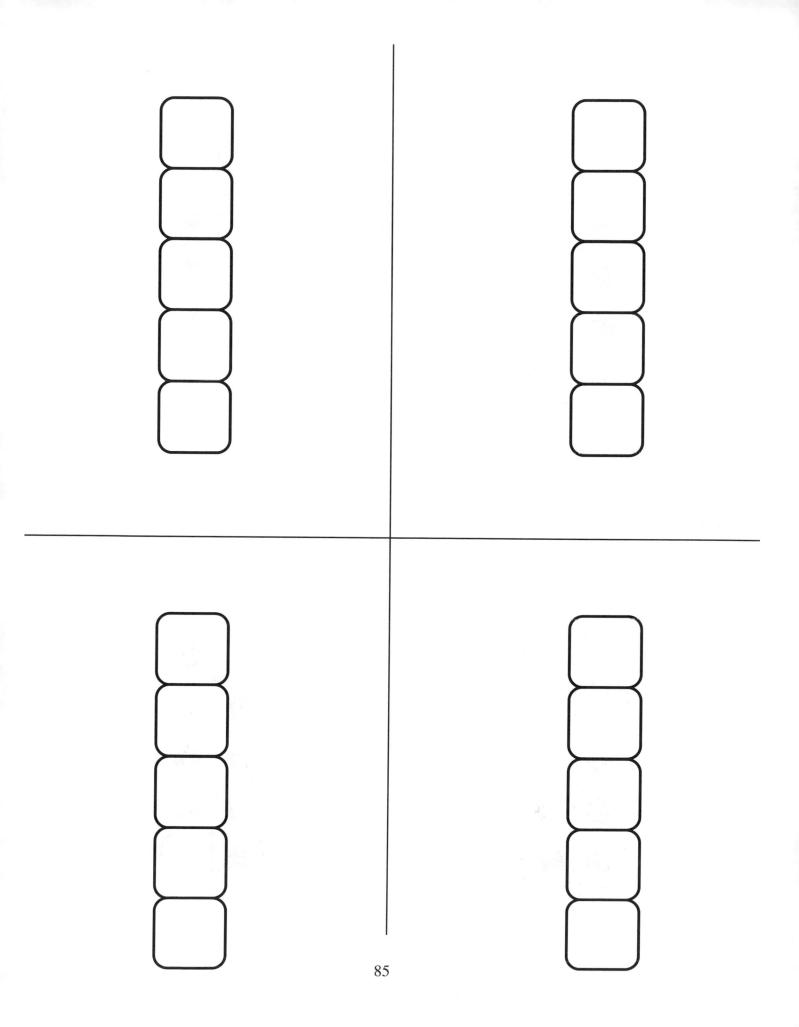

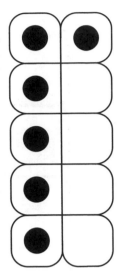 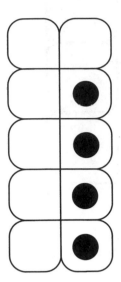

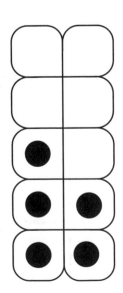 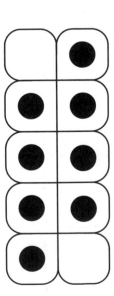

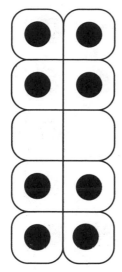

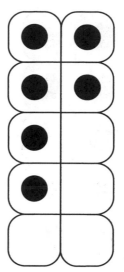

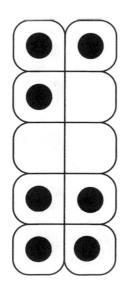

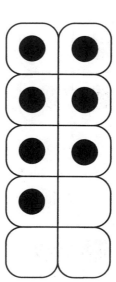

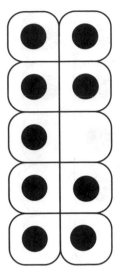

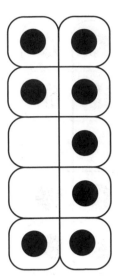

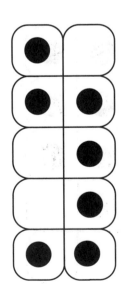

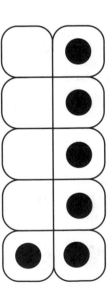

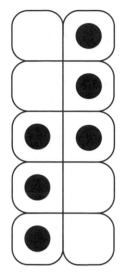

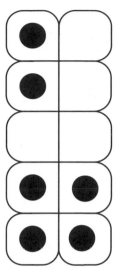

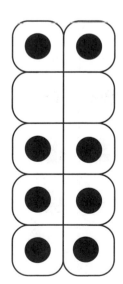

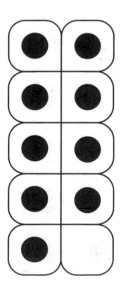

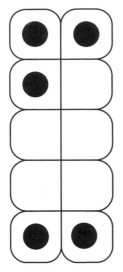

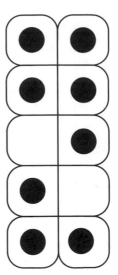

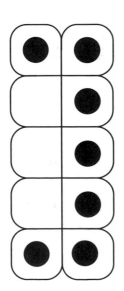

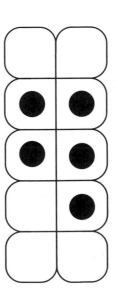

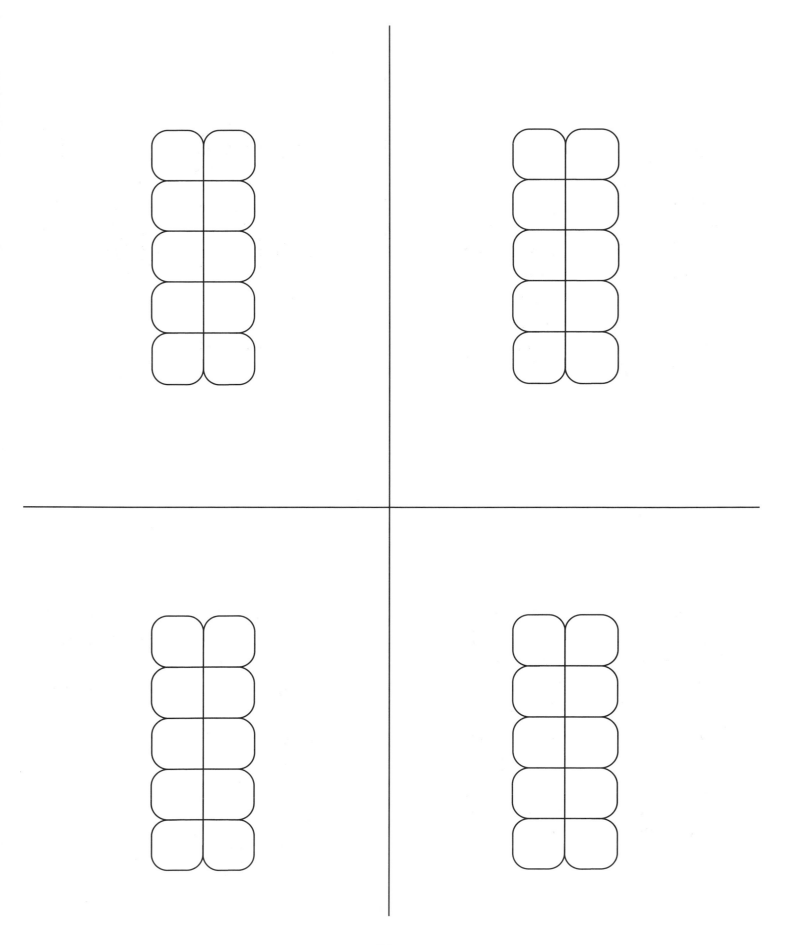

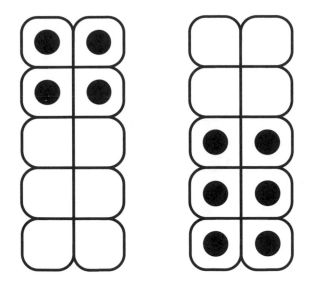

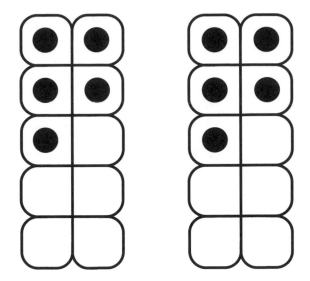

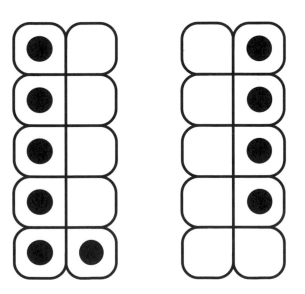

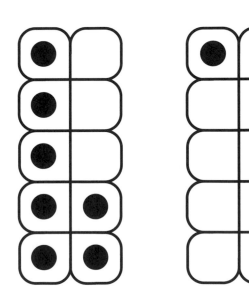

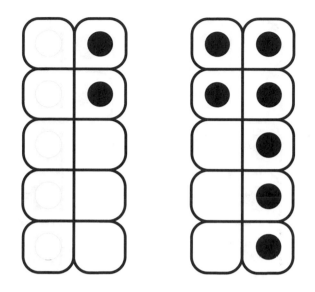

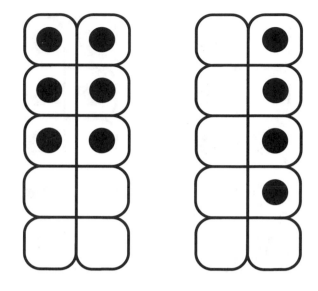

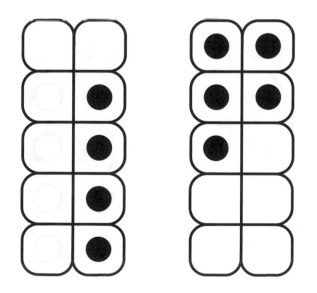

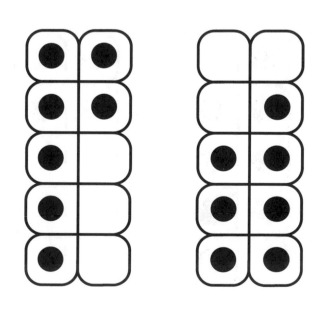

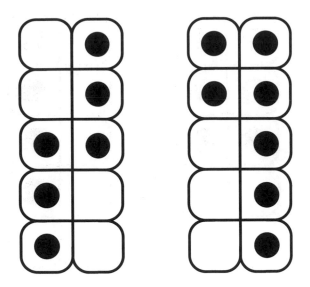

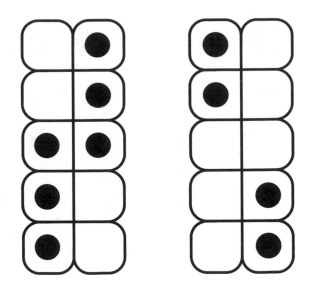

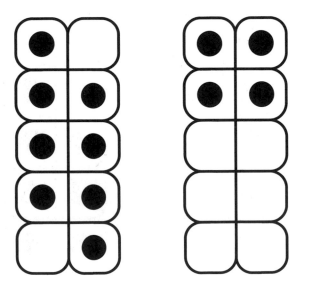

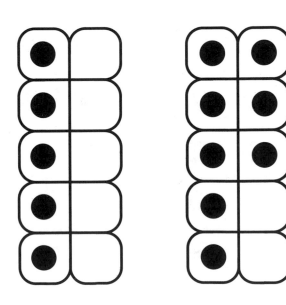

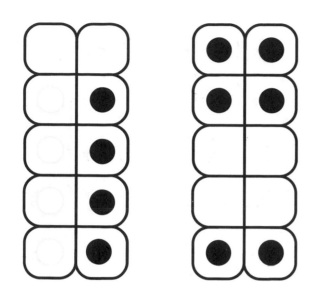

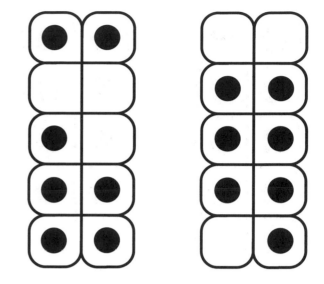

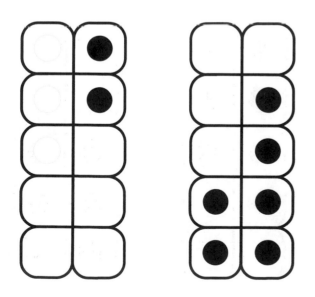

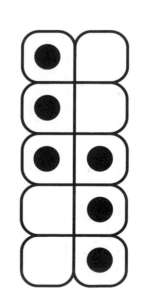

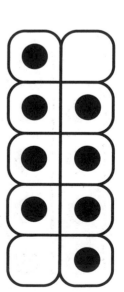

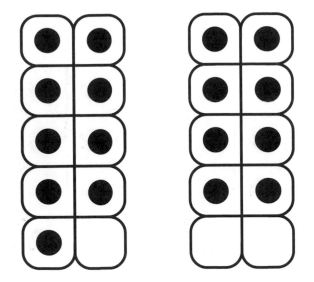

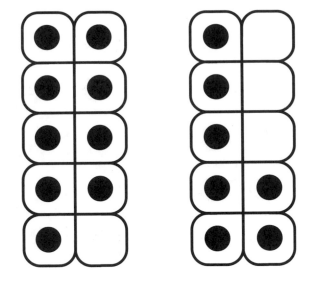

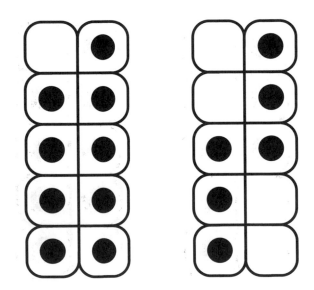

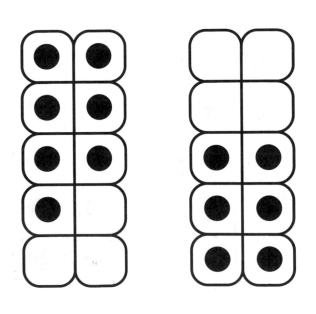

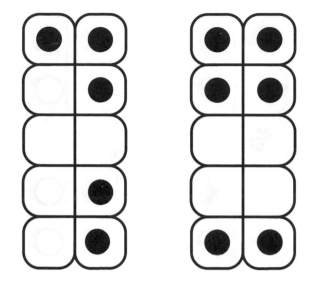

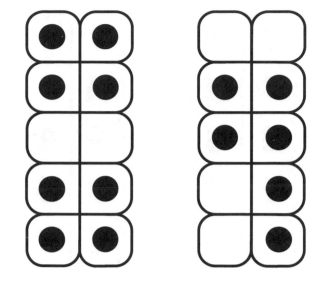

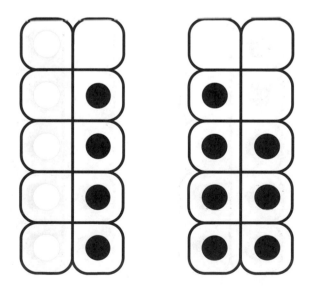

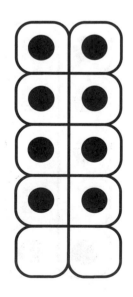 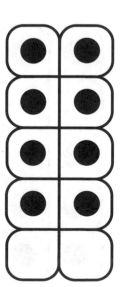

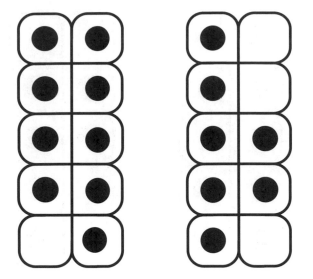

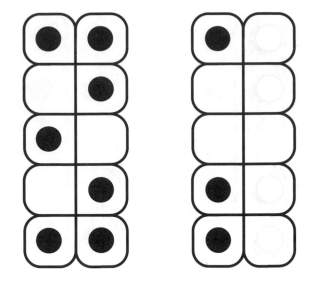

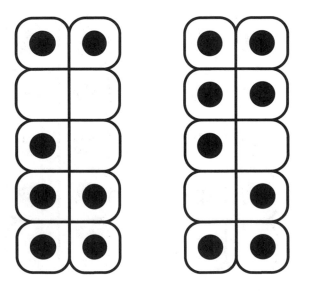

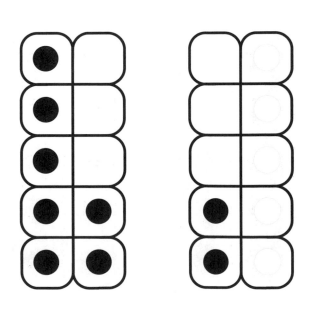

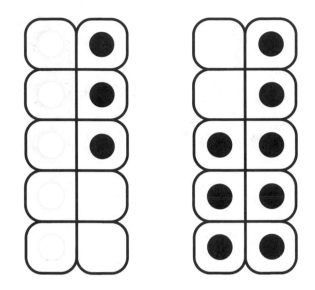

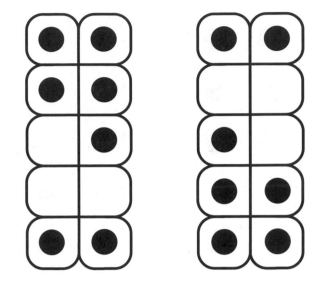

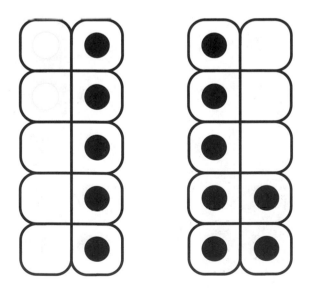

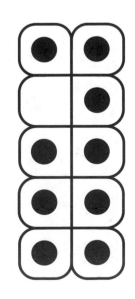

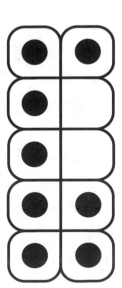

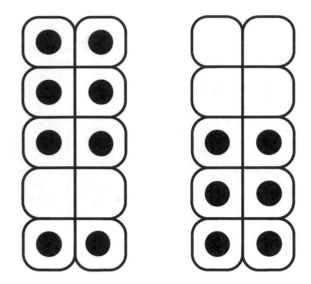

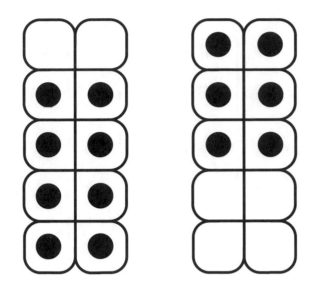

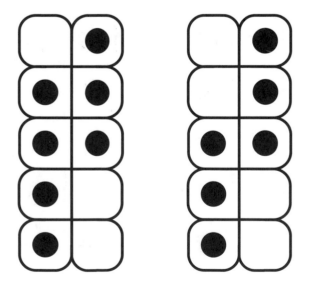

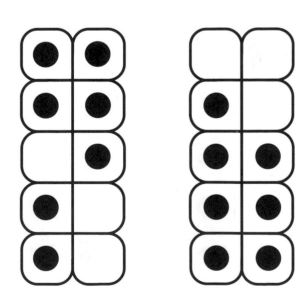

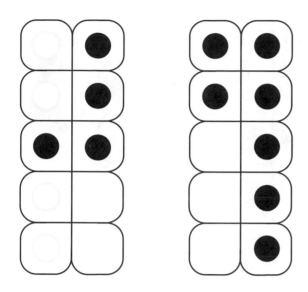

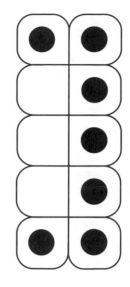

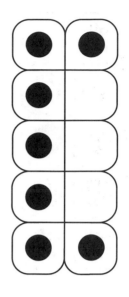

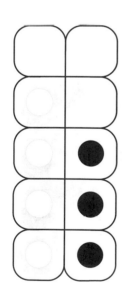

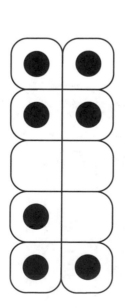

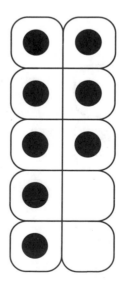

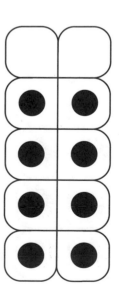

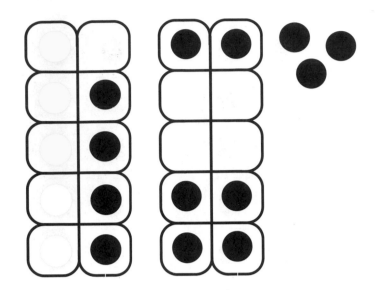

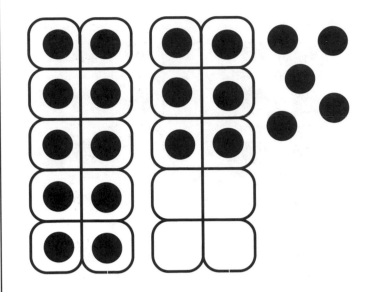

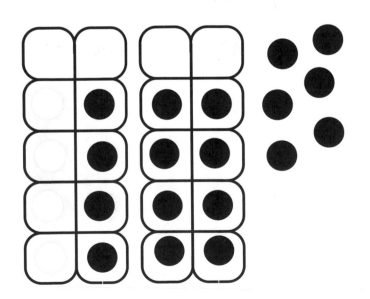

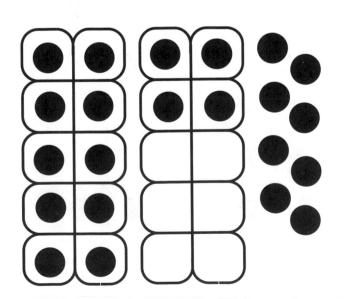

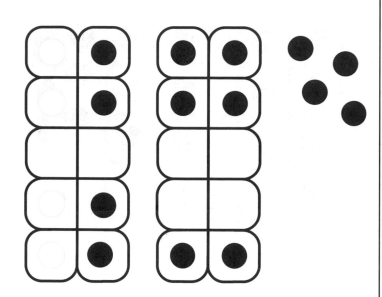

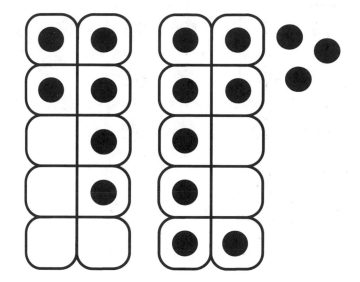

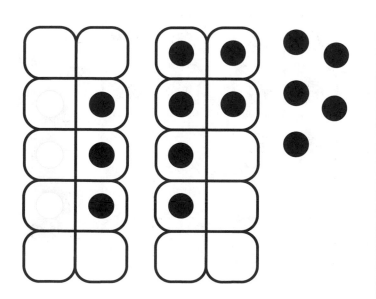

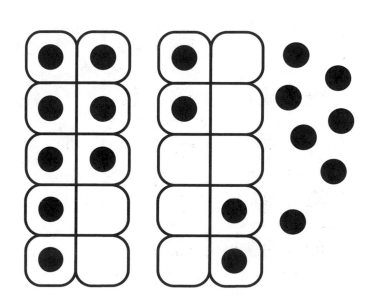

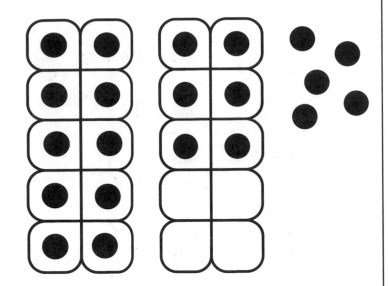

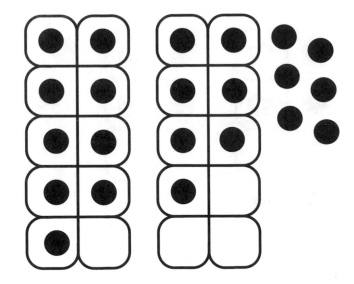

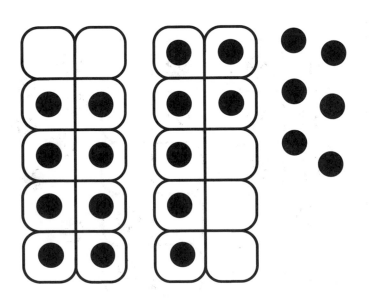

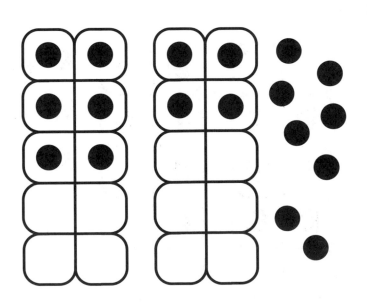

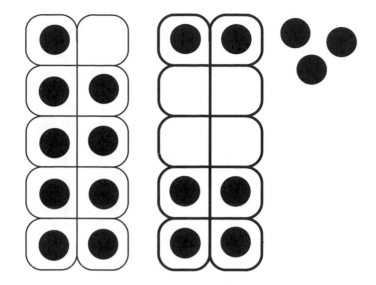 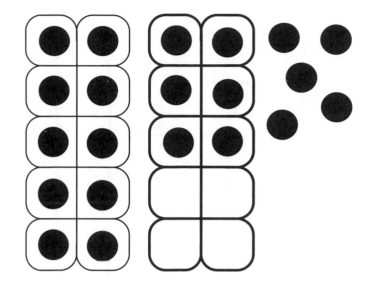

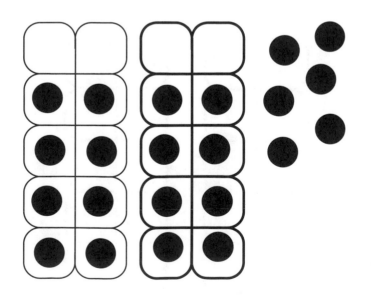 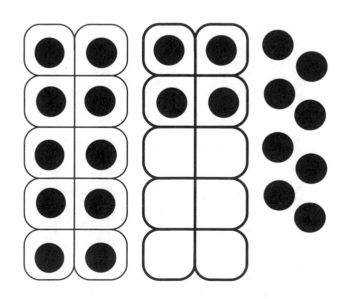

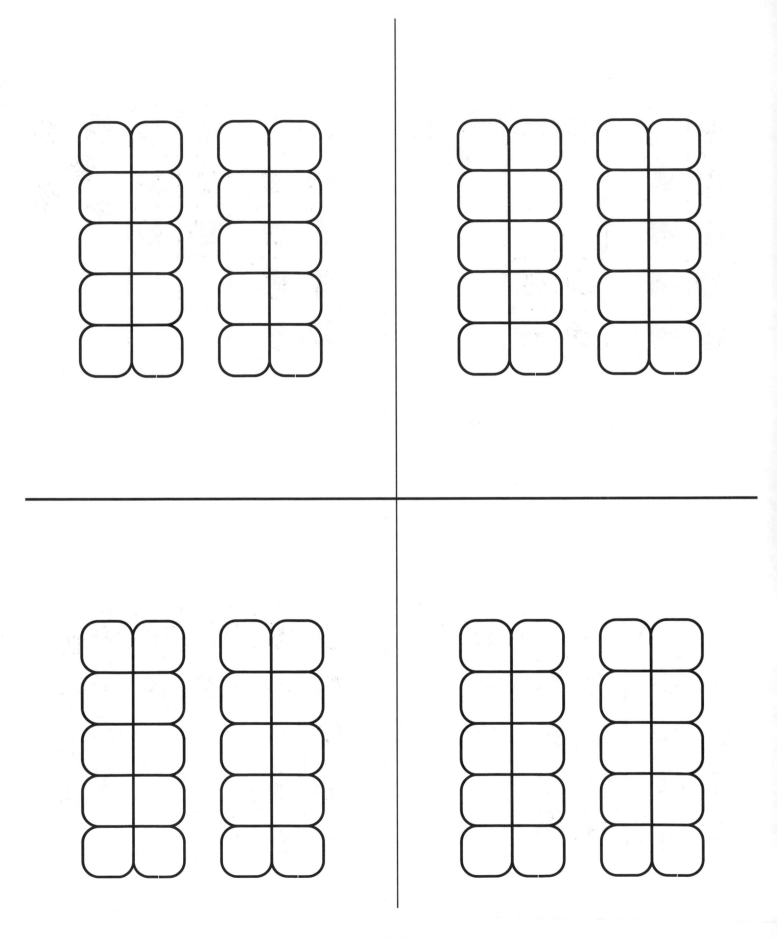

Balance Tasks

The nature of activities designed for mathematics learning influences the way students create their knowledge. If students normally experience addition and subtraction in abstract symbols set up vertically, their orientation may become highly procedural and they may fail to conceptualize addition and subtraction as meaningful mathematical operations. Even when students have addition presented horizontally as 5 + 6 = __ , many interpret = as "write the answer" and will often respond to 13 = 7 + __ with 20. Mathematics instruction is most effective when students experience ideas in a setting that is potentially meaningful to them - in a setting where they are encouraged to give meaning to their experiences rather than follow set procedures. Thus students should experience mathematics in a variety of settings which encourage sense making.

One setting that has proven effective in helping students conceptualize addition and subtraction is a balance scale. Balance is experienced naturally by each person in many situations. For example, the act of walking or riding a bicycle is a balancing act. Balancing is a bodily experience. Thus, students can easily give meaning to tasks presented in a balance format. Balance tasks must be interpreted, given meaning, and do not lend themselves to mechanical responses and thus encourage meaning making. Since no operation sign is provided, students must decide how to act, what operation to perform, and how to think about the task. It is useful to think of weights being placed on the two sides of the balance scale to make it balance. It could be helpful to have a pan balance in the classroom and have students experience putting blocks or other uniform objects on the scale to see the scale arm move and balance achieved. This is not necessary but could be used with students who may not immediately given meaning to the balance scale.

Note that a variety of arrangements are possible in putting weights on the balance. For example, the two balances shown on the side

107

must each be interpreted. In the first Balance, the unknown is the sum of 3 and 4 which can be obtained by adding. It could be symbolized as 4 + 3 = __ . The second Balance shown requires subtraction. One could think what could be put with 3 to balance 7. This might be symbolized as 7 = 3 + __ . In designing the balance activities, arrangements are varied intentionally with the largest number sometimes on the right and sometimes on the left. The four problems on a page have been carefully designed to encourage students to relate their thinking on one problem to another. We can think of mathematics as a rich network of concepts, relationships and self-generated procedures.

Because we are thinking in terms of weights, it obviously does not matter whether the two numbers on a side are interchanged, four and three is clearly the same weight as three and four. Thus the commutative property of addition becomes obvious. Students naturally construct commutitivity of addition as a relationship without any need for the term commutative.

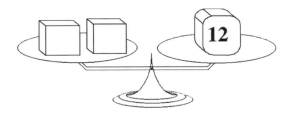

We adopt the convention that if the same number is to go in two boxes they will be identical. Thus in the figure shown at the side, six would go in each box rather than five and seven. This practice is a first step toward algebraic reasoning. In fact, the balance format encourages thinking in equations. The number sentence __ + 5 = 9 is not unlike the linear equations that are the focus of an algebra I course in high school where it would be written as x + 5 = 9. It is helpful to have students write number sentences for balances they have solved. It would not be stretching the truth to say that first graders who solve the balance tasks above are "doing" algebra.

In using the Balance tasks, it is important for students to develop their own ways of completing the activities. Some students may initially use objects in deciding how to fill the boxes. Others may refer to a hundreds board or some other material to solve the problem. Other students may use a counting strategy without

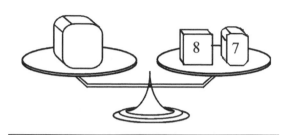

" I know that 8 and 8 are 16;
7 is one less so it must be 15."

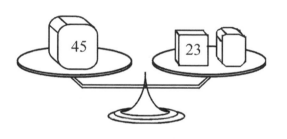

Anne: "23 and another ten makes
33, and another 10 makes 43 and
I need 2 more, so 10 and 10
make 20 and 2 is 22."

Arleshia: "I said 45 take away 20
is 25, and take away another 3 is
22."

manipulatives while others will use thinking strategies such as compensation (3 and 4 is seven because 3 and 3 is 6 and one more is seven - a doubles plus one strategy). The main goal of the balance activities is for students to develop their own meaningful ways of thinking about adding and subtracting and to develop thinking strategies. The final three Balance pages provide opportunities for students to construct algebraic concepts and to begin to symbolize problems in algebraic notation. As suggested for the other balance problems, have students write an equation that expresses the relationship. This should be done AFTER they have solved the problem. The goal is sense making and writing equations helps students to begin using abstract notation.

Using the balances with your class

After a brief discussion of Balances and perhaps a demonstration of a balance scale, present a Balance task, have students solve it and have them explain their thinking. Then arrange students in pairs and give each pair one balance sheet to complete. The students working in pairs are to discuss the problems and come to an agreement, if possible, on how to fill the boxes. This collaborative setting gives each student an opportunity to think through relationships and develop methods that make sense to him or her. Cobb has shown that learning occurs when there is disagreement in a pair and they negotiate their positions. So remember, when two students disagree there is rich potential for learning. You may want to have two or three Balance sheets available on a given day. When a pair has completed one page, you could give them a second one to consider. It is also wise to have a challenge page (more challenging balance tasks) for students who finish quickly and have developed good strategies. During this time, the goal is not to complete all the problems but to be actively engaged in thinking about the tasks – speed is not the goal.

Following the collaborative activity, bring the class together for a whole class discussion of the problems. You may wish to gather the students on the floor around a chalkboard or overhead projector. Have students present their solution methods to the class. Providing an opportunity for students to explain and justify their reasoning is an important component of math learning. Encourage students to question presenters when they do not understand or if they disagree. These whole class discussions are important for individual learning, developing an intellectual community in the classroom and providing you with much information about the students' thinking.

When students are working in pairs it is an excellent opportunity to think about how they are reasoning and interacting. You will be able to learn about the mathematical thinking of individual students and note information for assessment. These observations will also provide you with information on the variety of strategies being used by students. This will help you structure the whole class discussion so that relevant and important mathematics becomes the focus at that time. For example, it might be that most students have been solving each balance task on a page as a "new" task, not relating one task with another. However, you notice that Mary and Jim solved a balance task 7, __ ^ 17, arriving at 10 as their answer. Then, in solving the next problem, __ , 12 ^ 17 they used their previous result: "12 is 2 more than 10 so it has to be 2 less than 7, so it is 5." You can select that task as the focus for the whole class discussion, so that Mary and Jim's "different" strategy can provide opportunities for others to question and discuss this method. You can also be prepared to bring it into the discussion if necessary by inviting Mary and Jim to share their method.

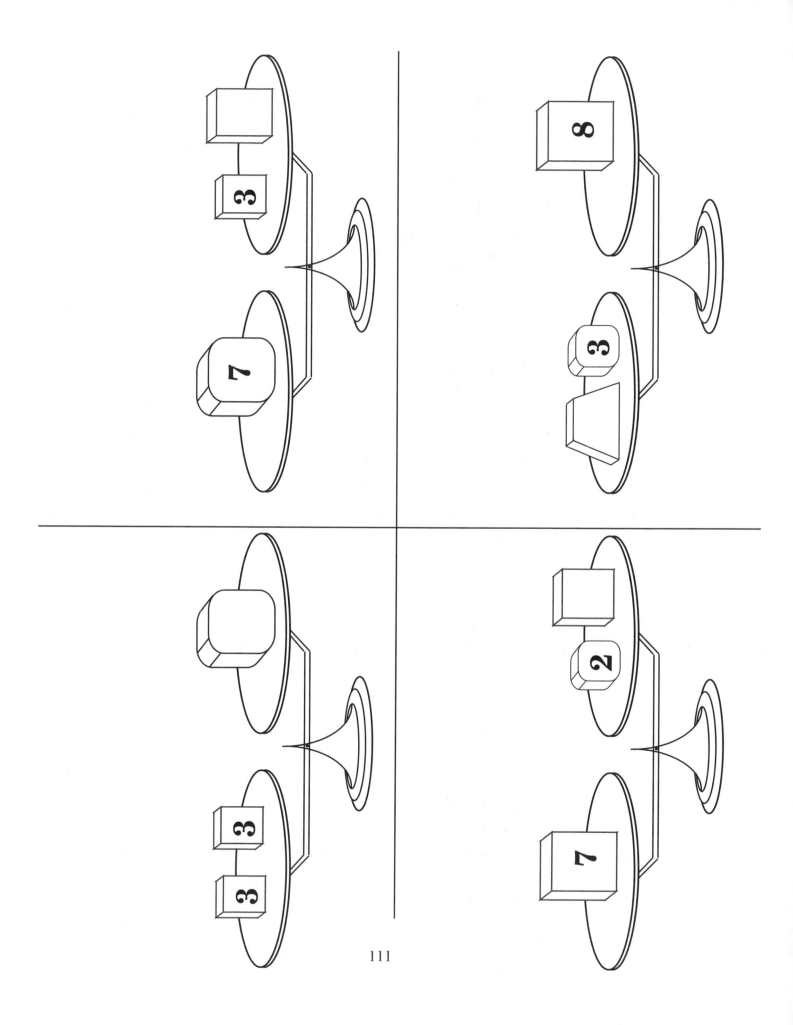

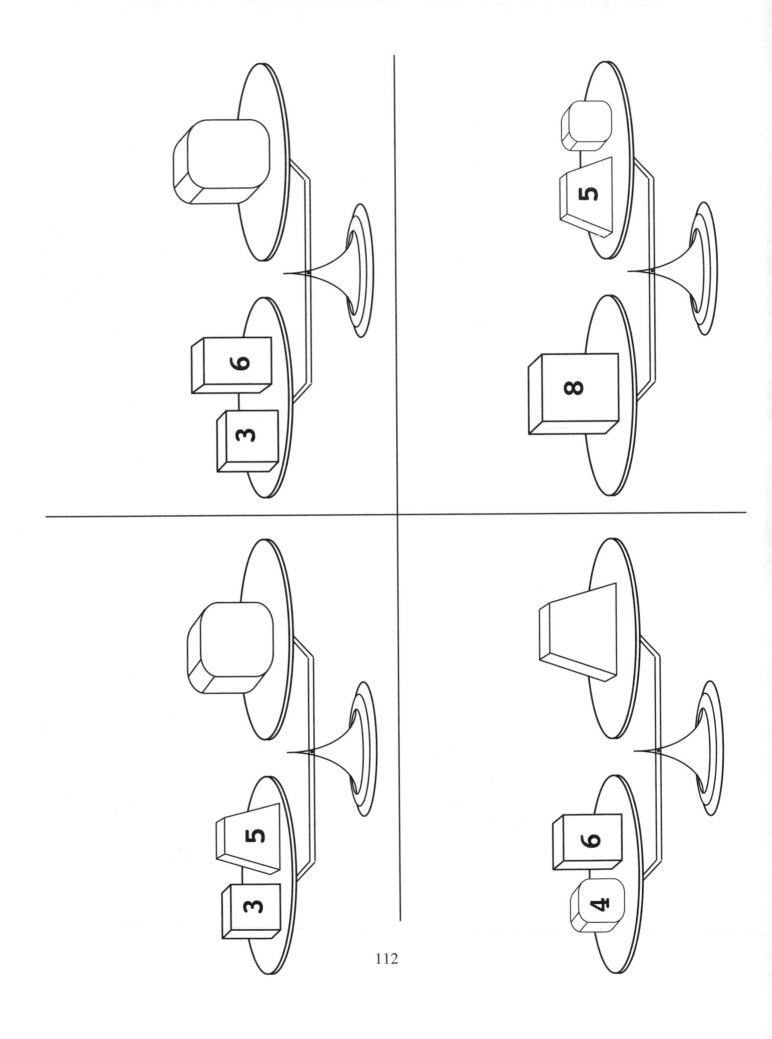

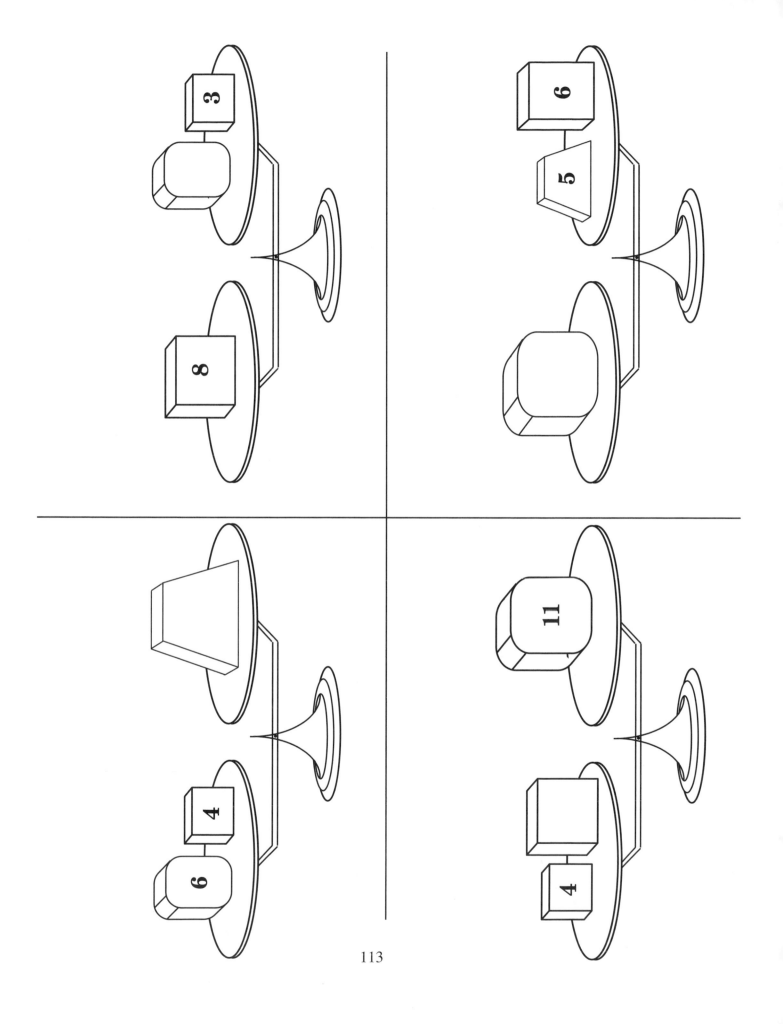

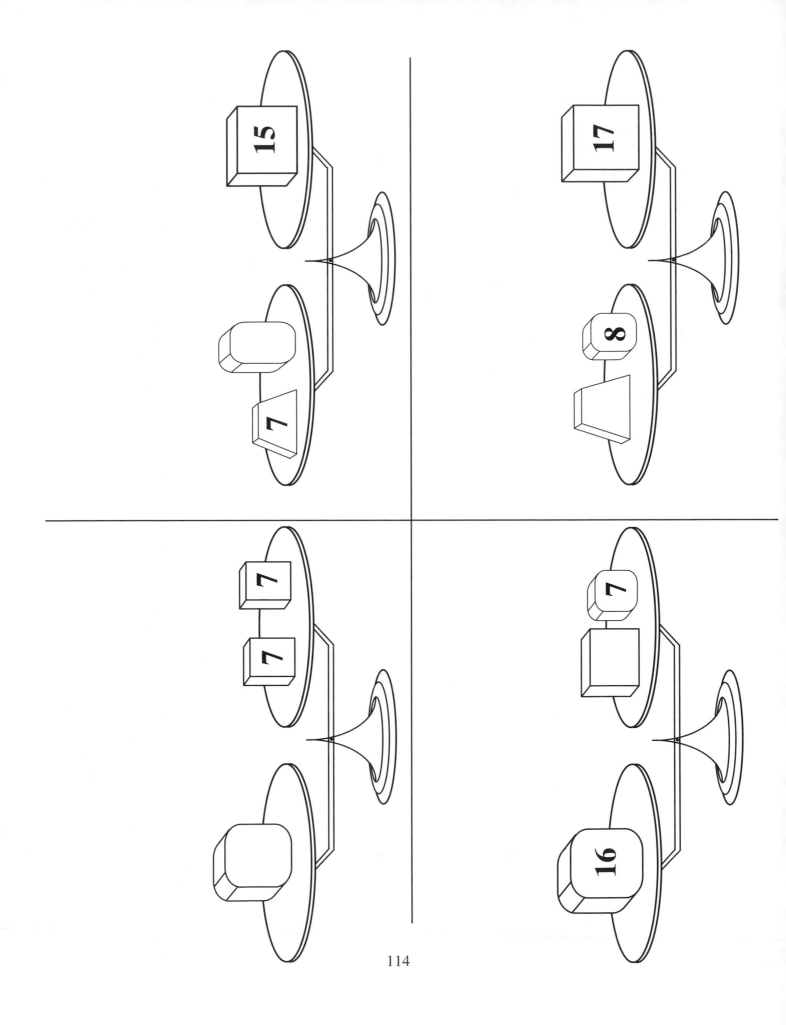

114

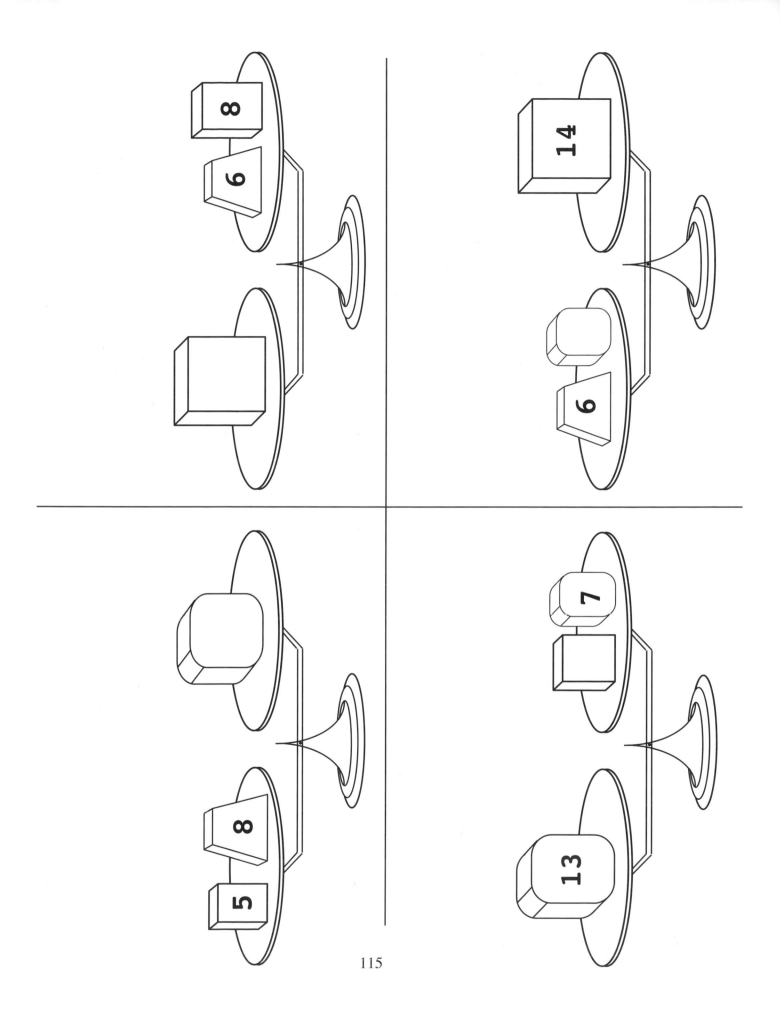

115

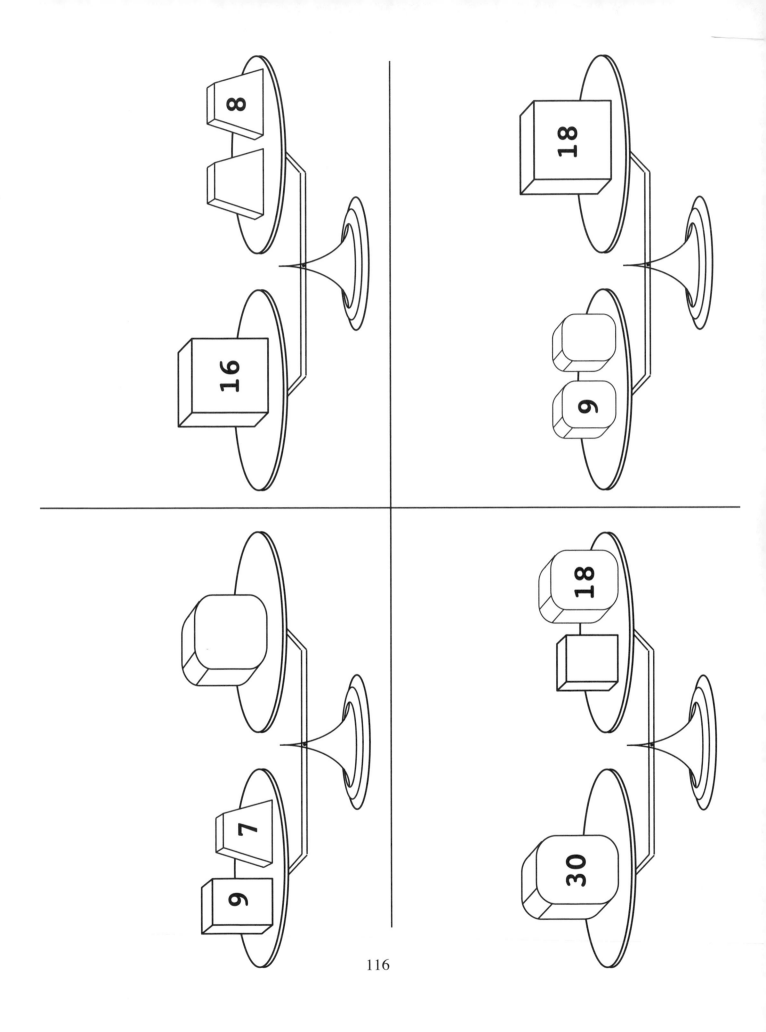

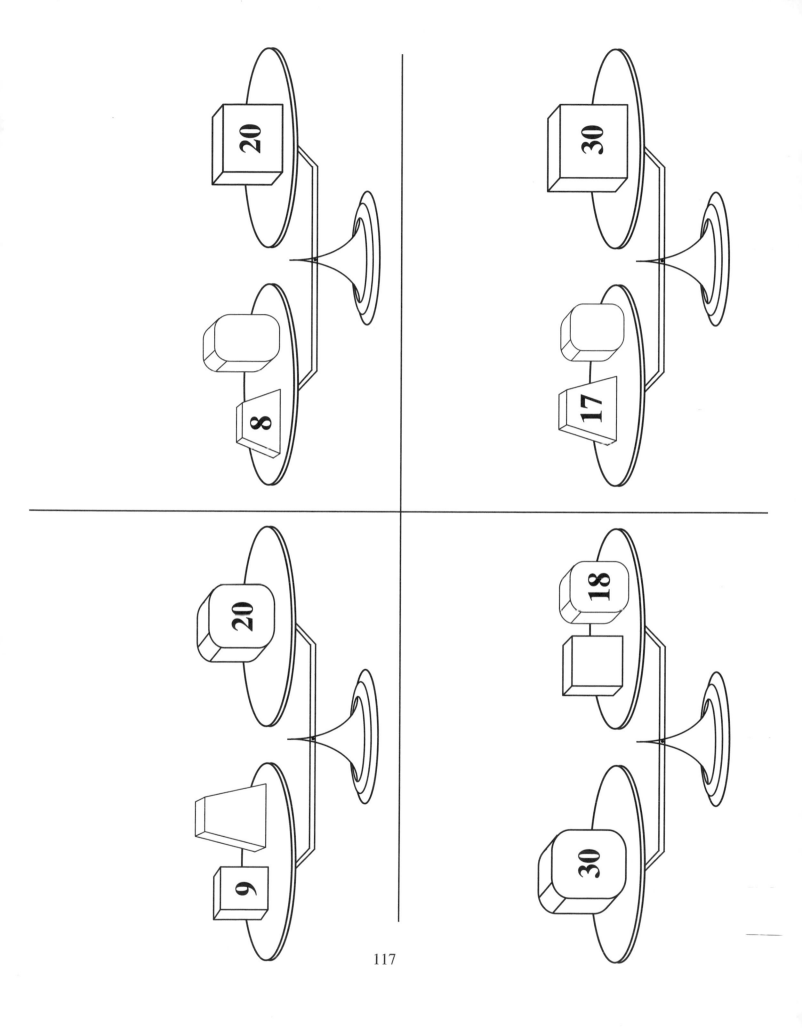

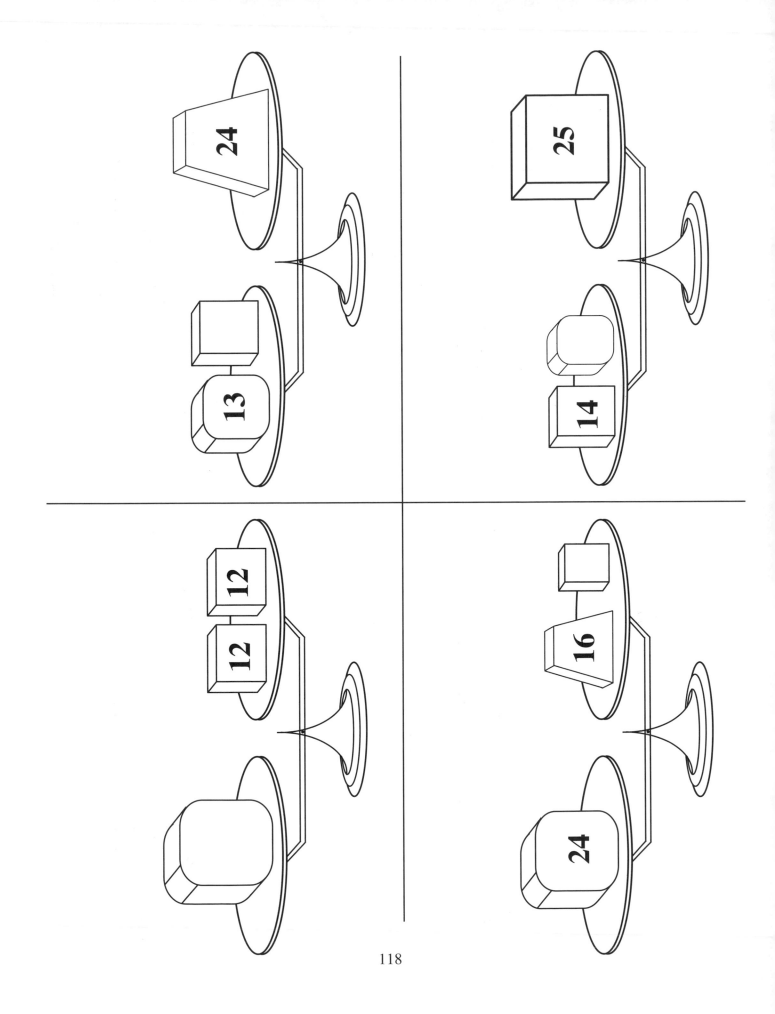

118

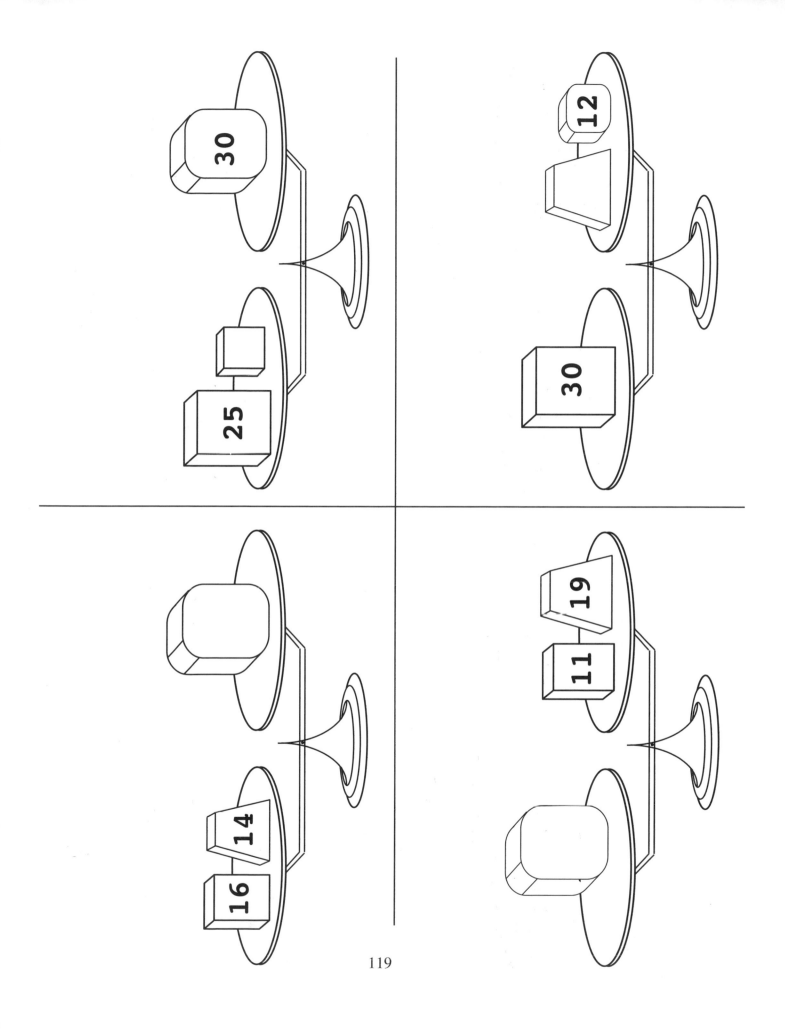

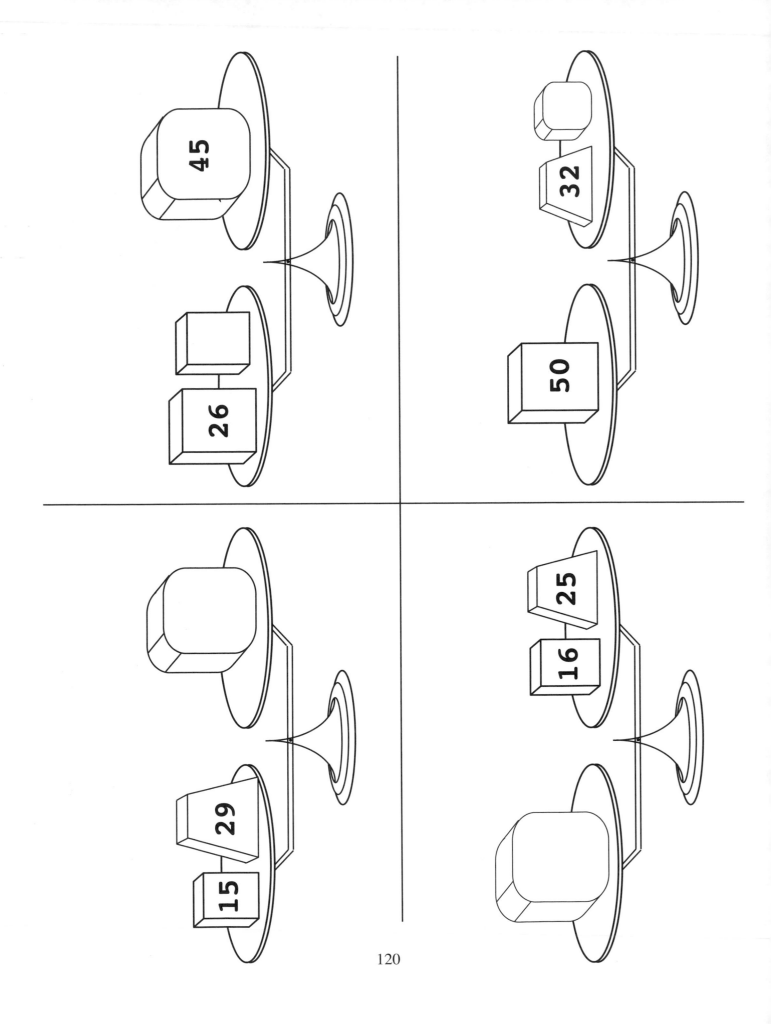

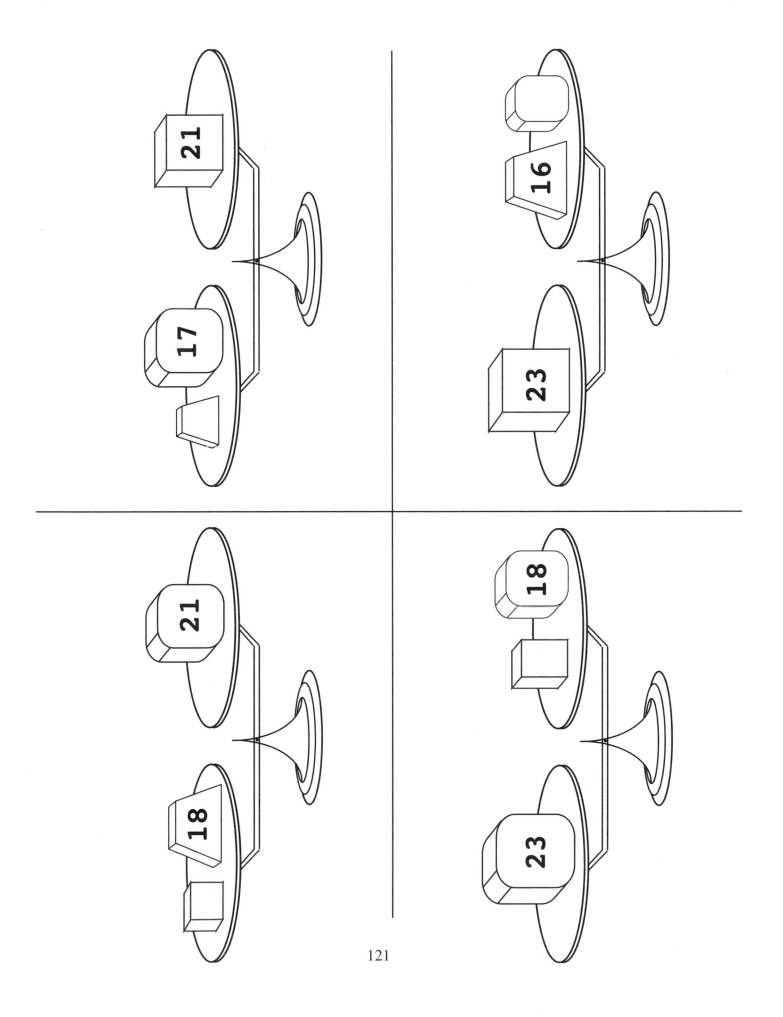

121

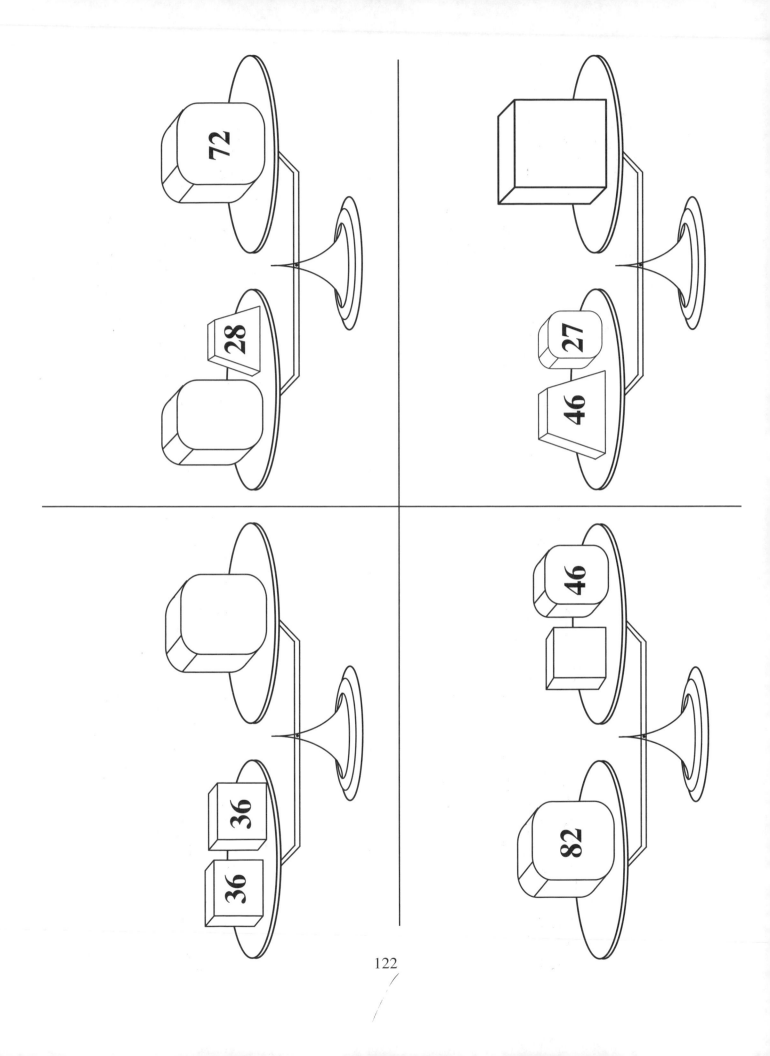

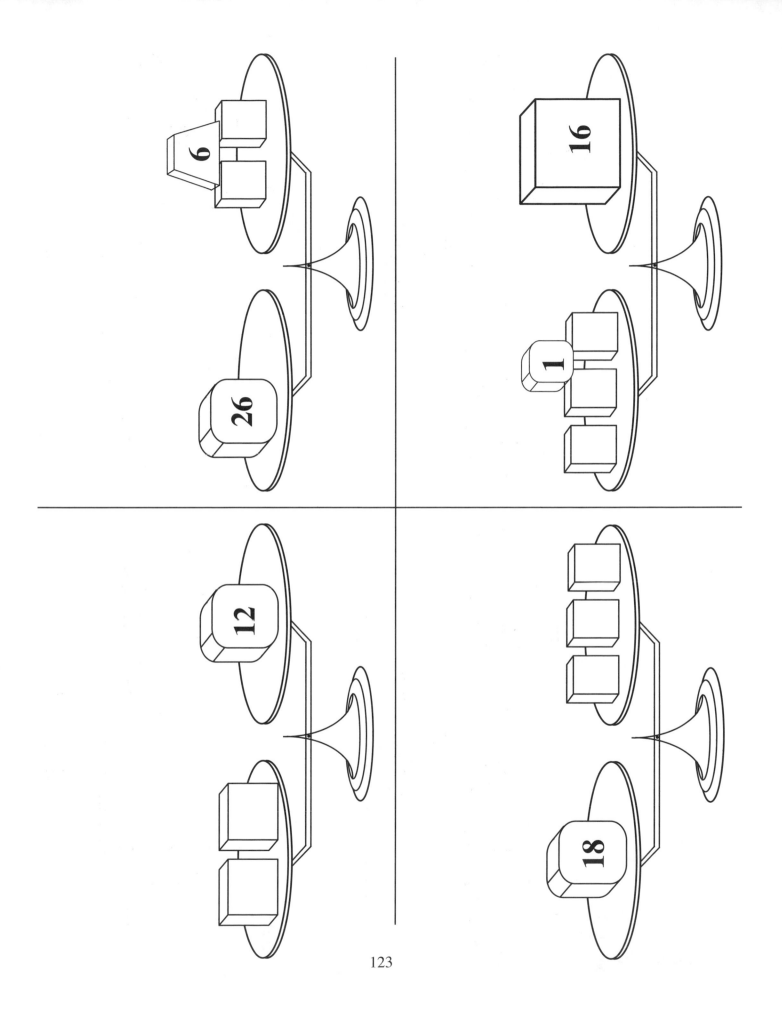

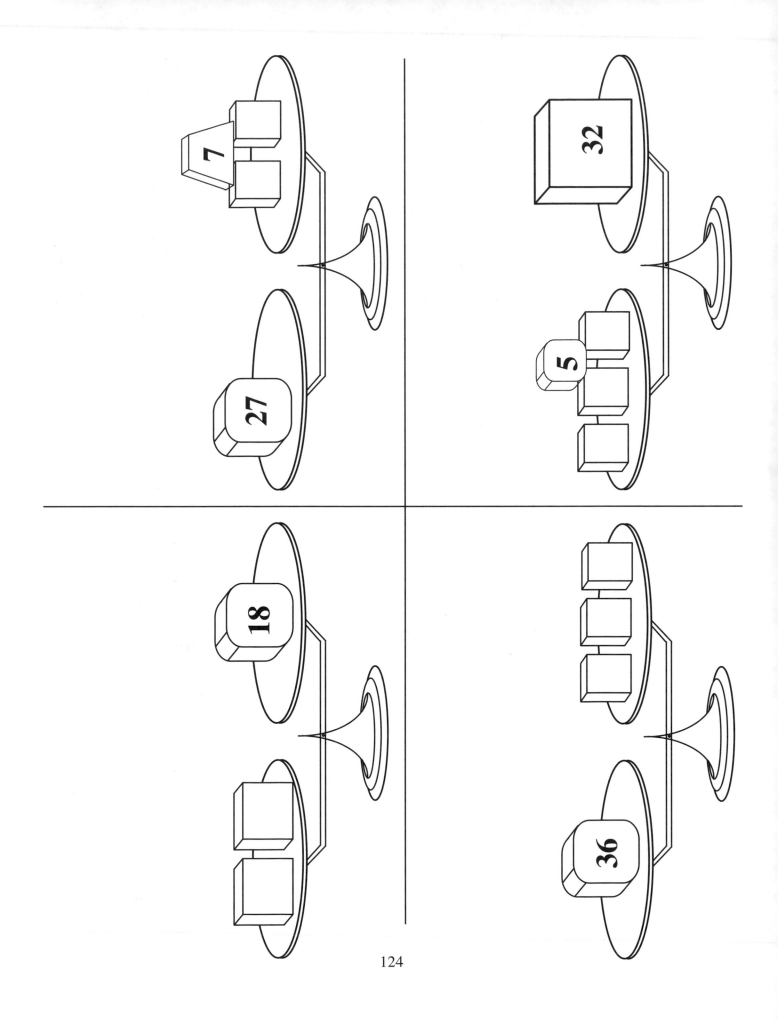

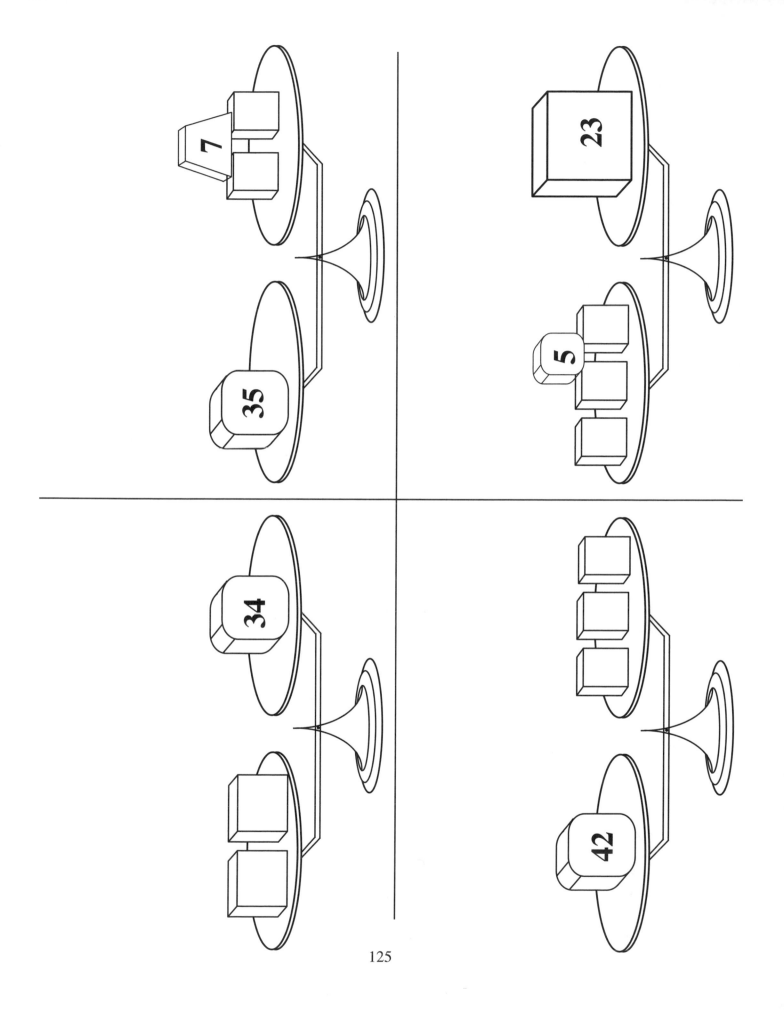

125

1	2	3	4	5	6	7	8	9	10
11	12	13	14	15	16	17	18	19	20
21	22	23	24	25	26	27	28	29	30
31	32	33	34	35	36	37	38	39	40
41	42	43	44	45	46	47	48	49	50
51	52	53	54	55	56	57	58	59	60
61	62	63	64	65	66	67	68	69	70
71	72	73	74	75	76	77	78	79	80
81	82	83	84	85	86	87	88	89	90
91	92	93	94	95	96	97	98	99	100

46 - 28

Dan: "This is 28, so I went down one, 38, then another one 48, then back 2, 46. So 46 − 28 is 18.

Suzy: "I thought if it was down 10 and then 1,2,3,4, 5,6,7,8 and 10 + 8 is 18."

Hal: "28 and 20 is 48 so 2 less is 46: 20 minus 2 is 18."

Our numeration system is based on ten and powers of ten such as a hundred, thousand and ten thousand. Coming to know "hundred" in a meaningful way is actually quite complex. We say students have constructed a hundred as a mathematical object when they can think of it simultaneously as one thing (hundred), hundred things, or ten tens. Coordinating ones, tens and hundreds is an important accomplishment in coming to know number. One hundred can become a unit with which to think along with five and ten; they become mental landmarks.

Coming to know the numbers from one to one hundred involves making, in a mental sense, the landmarks of 10, 20, 30, 40, 50, 60, 70, 80, and 90. To a second grader, 37 may have little meaning other than a word said in counting. Or it may be thought of as a collection of 37 single objects. When it becomes related to 27 and 47, the student has made significant progress in coming to know 37. Some students may think of 37 as having a ten part and ones part but still not have a sense of 37 as a number of objects. For example, when asked to count out 16 objects and write the numeral for that number and then asked to "Show what this means (pointing to the 1 of 16)" students will often indicate a single object in the set. These students may be able to say that 37 is three tens and seven and yet not have constructed it as a number in a deeper sense, the three tens and seven ones may not be coordinated. Until students can coordinate tens and ones their reasoning will be limited. When asked "What is ten more than 27?" these same students will count by ones, indicating that, for them, 37 is unrelated to 17, 27, and 47.

The hundreds board can help students learn to coordinate tens and ones so that two-digit numerals have mathematical meaning related to other numbers. Working on a hundreds board to add and subtract two-digit numbers provides opportunities for students to construct many number patterns which can be useful in using numbers in meaningful settings. Because 7, 17, 27, 37, . . . are aligned under each other in a column. The opportunity exists for students to relate them as "ten more." When adding 26 and 17 on a hundreds board, students may at first count-on from the 26 seventeen times and take the number under their finger at that point as the answer. In the process of doing so, they have the opportunity to realize that by moving down one space they are adding ten so they might say 26, 36, 37, 38, 39, 40, 41, 42, 43, . . . 43. While still an inefficient way of adding 26 and 17, the activity can help students think of two-digit numerals as names for numbers that are in a sequence from one to one hundred, intimately related to each other.

Students can come to use a numbered hundreds board in a mechanical way and not construct more abstract ways of reasoning. Using a blank hundreds frame can help students move beyond a procedural counting-on strategy to constructing abstract number patterns and relationships. You may also want to have a hundreds chart in the classroom.

When hundreds boards are available for students to use in their number activity, the following procedures have been found to help them construct meaning of numbers and think in tens.

Give each student a blank hundreds board with just the numbers 1 and 2 in position. Have students write the numbers on their hundreds boards. Encourage them to find patterns as they fill in all spaces on thier hundreds board. Conclude with a whole class discussion of the various patterns students noticed as they were completing the hundreds board.

Make an overhead transparency of a blank hundreds board. Place a penny on one of the squares of the board and ask students to figure out the number that should be written there. Have students share the different ways they used to decide the number that should be in that place on the board. This activity can be used as a class opener one or two days each week.

Duplicate the following activity sheets and have students work in pairs to complete them in preparation for class discussion. The class discussion is an integral part of the lesson. Have students describe the ways they reasoned in filling in empty squares.

Thousands Books. When you feel students are getting comfortable thinking in tens, have them make a thousands book. Distribute 10 blank hundreds grids to each student and have them write the numbers from one to 100 on the first, 101 to

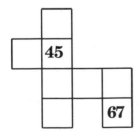

200 on the next and so on. This may take several class periods to be completed. You may wish the students to complete this activity at home. Once completed, have each student design a cover and make their Thousands Book. These can be kept on the shelf for reference when working with three digit numbers. This activity helps students give meaning the numbers such as 538. They can form a mental image from their thousands book experience and think of 538 as being on the fifth sheet down and in the 38 position. Many students go through elementary school without giving meaning to numbers in the hundreds. They may become proficient with procedures for adding and subtracting such symbols but not have any mathematical idea what they are doing. Just as students need opportunities to construct meaning for the numbers from one to ten and then to a hundred, they also need opportunities to construct meaning for the numbers in the hundreds.

Hundreds Board

1	2	3	4	5	6	7	8	9	10
11	12	13	14	15	16	17	18	19	20
21	22	23	24	25	26	27	28	29	30
31	32	33	34	35	36	37	38	39	40
41	42	43	44	45	46	47	48	49	50
51	52	53	54	55	56	57	58	59	60
61	62	63	64	65	66	67	68	69	70
71	72	73	74	75	76	77	78	79	80
81	82	83	84	85	86	87	88	89	90
91	92	93	94	95	96	97	98	99	100

Hundreds Boards

1	2	3	4	5	6	7	8	9	10
11	12	13	14	15	16	17	18	19	20
21	22	23	24	25	26	27	28	29	30
31	32	33	34	35	36	37	38	39	40
41	42	43	44	45	46	47	48	49	50
51	52	53	54	55	56	57	58	59	60
61	62	63	64	65	66	67	68	69	70
71	72	73	74	75	76	77	78	79	80
81	82	83	84	85	86	87	88	89	90
91	92	93	94	95	96	97	98	99	100

1	2	3	4	5	6	7	8	9	10
11		13	14	15	16	17	18		20
21	22	23		25	26		28	29	30
31		33	34	35	36	37		39	40
	42	43	44	45		47	48	49	50
51		53	54	55	56	57		59	60
61	62		64		66	67	68		
	72		74	75	76		78	79	80
81	82		84		86	87		89	90
91		93		95	96	97	98	99	100

Hundreds Boards

31	32	33	34	35	36	37	38	39	40
					46				
							78		

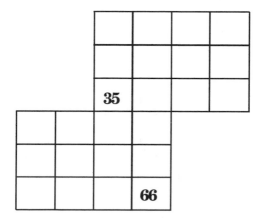

133

Hundreds Boards

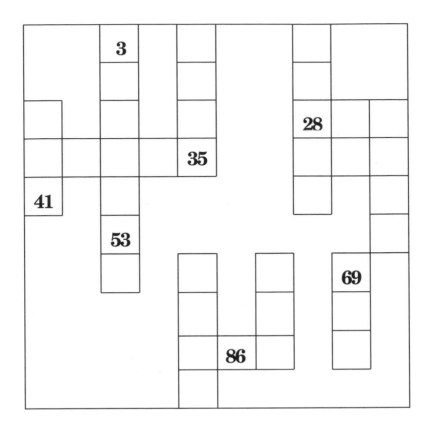

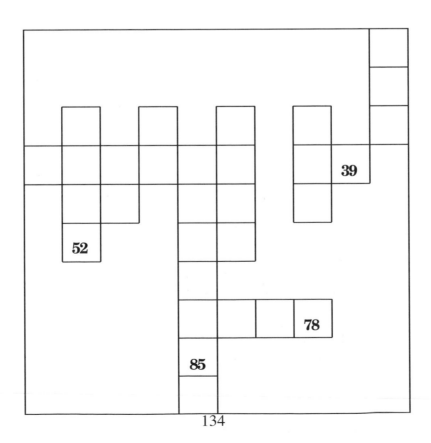

Hundreds Boards

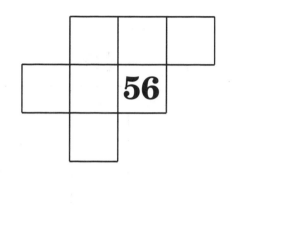

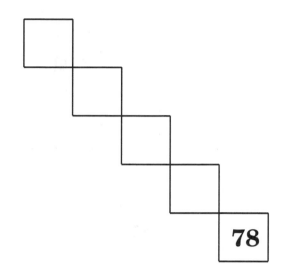

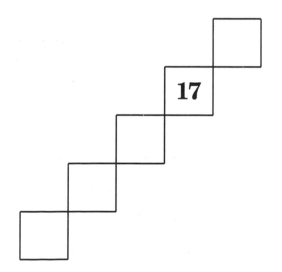

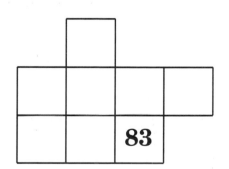

Hundreds Boards

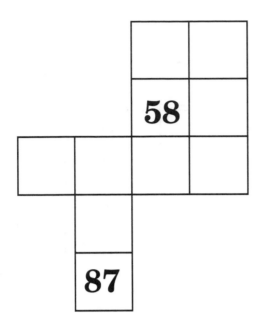

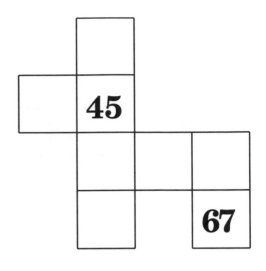

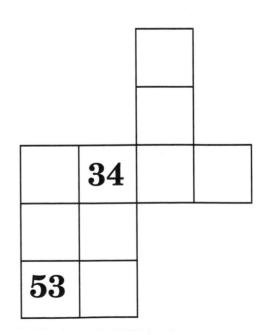

Thousands Book master page to be duplicated, 10 for each student.

Math Squares

Coming to know number is more than memorizing facts and practicing demonstrated procedures. The purpose of Math Squares is to provide opportunities for students to construct thinking strategies and their own meaningful ways of adding and subtracting. The emphasis is on mental arithmetic and building number patterns. The numbers can be chosen so that the activity is appropriate for students in any elementary school grade. Furthermore, knowledge of decimals, money, and integers can be engendered with Math Squares.

Notice that in Math Squares there are no operation or equal signs. Thus students must base their actions on reasoning about the situation. Rather than carrying out procedures which could be done without thinking, the student must decide which numbers to work with first and what to do with them. In all cases there are multiple ways of proceeding. The numbers are chosen to encourage the combining of compatible numbers and using ten as a mental benchmark. For example, 19 and 21 might be in diagonal rooms. While adding numbers in two rooms which are diagonal from each other might not be the first thought or most natural thing to do, it may greatly facilitate the solution process. Math Squares encourage students to think about their activity and do what makes sense rather than following fixed procedures.

19	7
6	21

———

Kieshia: "I took 19 and 21 and made it 20 and 20, so that's 40. Then I know that 7 and 7 is 14 so that's 54, but it was only 6 so it's 53."

Carlos: "I took one from the six and made it five. 19 and 1 is 20 and another 5 is 25. Then I added 21 and 7 to get 28. Then I had to add 25 and 28. I know that 25 and 25 is 50, but there's 3 more so it's 53."

Procedure:
Begin by presenting Math Squares as a whole class activity on the overhead or chalkboard.

"Here we have four rooms. We know how many people there are in each room. How many people are there altogether?" [For the second type: "Here we have four rooms. We know how many persons there are in all. How many persons are there in this room?"]

Have students describe how they found the total or missing number. Encourage a variety of ways. Ask students to explain their methods and any patterns they notice.

After introducing Math Squares as a whole class activity, have students work in pairs to fill the empty squares or find the sum if all squares are filled. Always follow the small group work with a whole class discussion where students explain their methods. You may wish to ask questions such as:

"Is there another way?"
"Which way do you like best?"
"Is there a method someone showed today that you might use?"

Math Squares

3	2
5	7

_____

8	9
	2

__20__

7	8
3	

__20__

9	2
8	

__30__

5	7
5	5

_____

4	8
	6

__28__

Math Squares

4	7
5	6

_____

4	7
3	

15

4	5
3	

16

8	5
5	2

_____

1	4
	9

19

2	
6	8

20

142

Math Squares

6	9
11	4

_____

8	9
	2

__40__

3	
17	7

__40__

9	19
1	2

_____

23	7
	8

__50__

12	12
12	12

_____

Math Squares

25	7
3	15

_____

35	6
4	15

_____

15	6
10	

__35__

35	8
	15

__60__

30	6
4	

__55__

32	6
4	

__55__

Math Squares

17	22
28	10

_____

33	27
	28

90

19	24
6	24

_____

30	31
19	

90

	19
11	25

55

9	14
16	

55

145

Math Squares

16	**9**
31	**14**

_____

8	**19**
	20

_____
50

7	**13**
	27

_____
50

8	**19**
	12

_____
50

	34
6	**18**

_____
68

17	
16	**8**

_____
45

146

Math Squares

41	35
16	19

_____

32	27
	28

50	26
8	

100

	35
15	19

100

75	50
50	75

_____

17	
21	63

100

147

Math Squares

175	150
250	25

_____

175	
24	50

__300__

	275
25	500

__1000__

60	700
	50

__1000__

325	
50	325

__1100__

475	125
275	

__1000__

Math Squares

170	175
275	30

_____

245	
25	50

__550__

	275
50	325

__900__

60	490
	50

__800__

280	
40	280

__700__

367	284
275	

__1000__

149

Math Squares

27.50	6.00
6.00	10.50

_____

15.50	24.75
5.25	

__50.00__

3.75	2.25
	1.50

__10.00__

1.25	
7.50	3.75

__60.00__

140.00	37.50
2.50	60.00

_____

	60.00
25.50	24.50

__130.00__

Math Squares

$\frac{1}{2}$	$\frac{1}{2}$
1	$\frac{1}{2}$

___

$\frac{1}{4}$	$\frac{1}{4}$
$\frac{1}{4}$	

2

$\frac{1}{2}$	$\frac{1}{4}$
$\frac{1}{4}$	$\frac{1}{2}$

___

$\frac{1}{4}$	**2**
2$\frac{1}{2}$	$\frac{3}{4}$

___

$\frac{1}{4}$	**2**
$\frac{1}{4}$	$\frac{1}{4}$

5

	$\frac{1}{2}$
$\frac{3}{4}$	$\frac{1}{4}$

4

Math Squares

$\frac{1}{2}$	**5**
4	$\frac{1}{2}$

——

$\frac{1}{4}$	$\frac{3}{4}$
$\frac{1}{4}$	

__**4**__

$5\frac{1}{2}$	**5**
9	$4\frac{1}{2}$

——

$2\frac{1}{4}$	**7**
8	$6\frac{3}{4}$

——

$\frac{1}{4}$	**2**
	$\frac{3}{4}$

__$5\frac{1}{4}$__

$\frac{3}{4}$	$\frac{1}{2}$
	$\frac{1}{4}$

__$4\frac{1}{2}$__

Two Ways

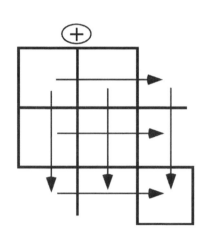

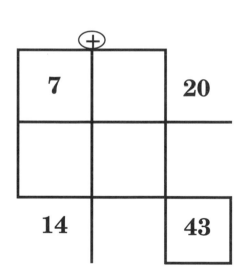

In Two Ways, the numbers in a row must add to a number at the right and the numbers in each column must add to a number at the bottom. Then the two numbers at the right must add to the number in the bottom right corner and the numbers along the bottom must also add the same number. These actions are indicated with arrows in the diagram shown.

Thus there is a self-check built into the design of the activity and it becomes a mathematical puzzle. Furthermore, by varying the position of the four given numbers, the activity takes on more of a problem solving nature and interrelates addition and subtraction. Of course if the four given numbers are all in the upper left, the solution is quite straight forward; students add across and then down. The numbers in the right and bottom margins should add to the same check number in the lower right corner.

In the example at the left, a decision where to start must be made. There are, in fact, four ways to begin this example. The square between 7 and 20 would have to be 13 (7 + _ = 20), the square between 7 and 14 would have to be 7 (7 + _ = 14), the square between 14 and 43 would be 29 (14 + _ = 43), and the square between 20 and 43 would be 23 (20 + _ = 43). With these numbers it is then possible to deduce that the space between 13 and 29 must be 16. But the 16 must also be the difference between 23 and 7 (horizontally) and thus a check is achieved. It was not possible to derive the 16 until other numbers had been determined.

Two Ways present opportunities for students to construct number relationships in an interesting setting that provides a self-check. It is surprising how much students enjoy the Two Way format. As students attempt to fill all the empty spaces in the various arrangements of given numbers, they will come to relate addition and subtraction. In completing a single Two Way, at least six computations must be performed so students are getting rich experiences when they solve a Two Way.

153

Two Ways

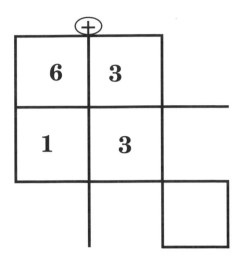

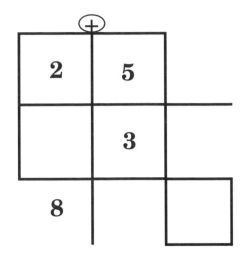

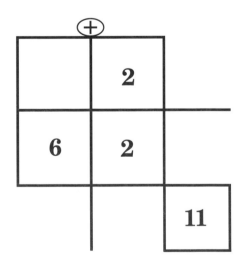

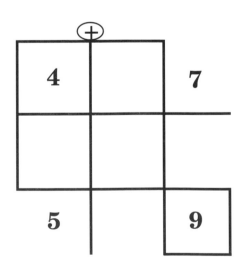

154

Two Ways

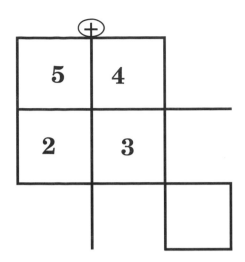

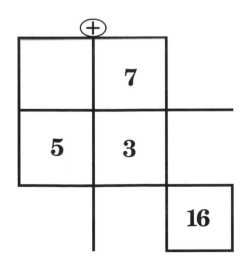

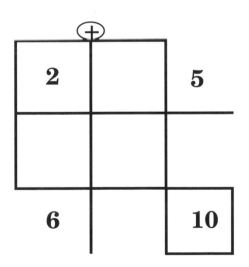

155

Two Ways

$\oplus$

7	5
8	6

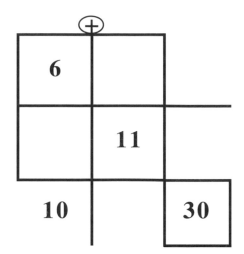

$\oplus$

6

8 | 12 | 9

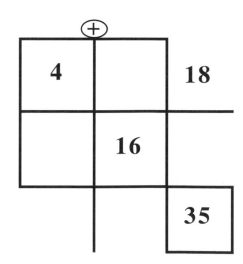

Two Ways

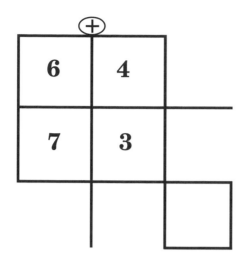

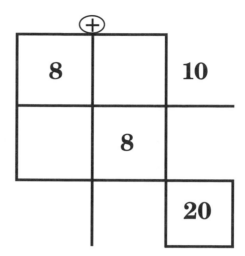

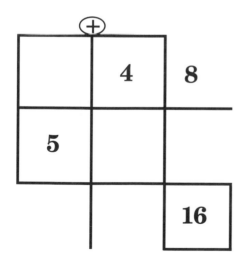

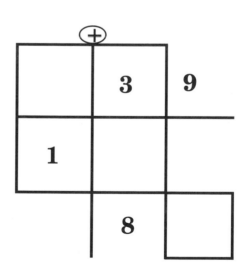

Two Ways

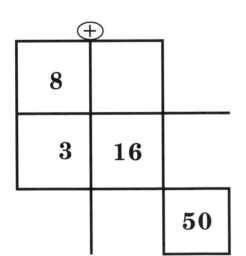

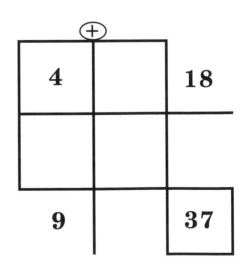

Two Ways

+	
6	14
19	5

+	
9	15
	17
20	

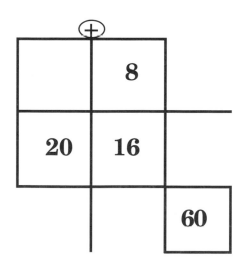

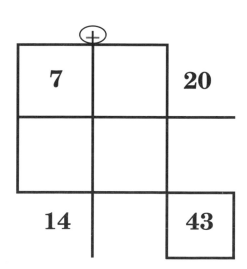

Two Ways

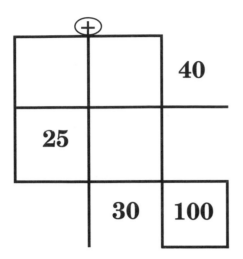

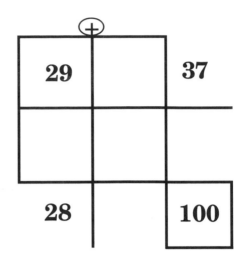

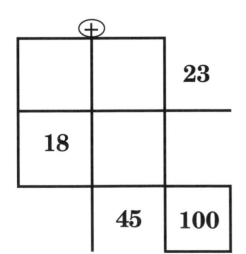

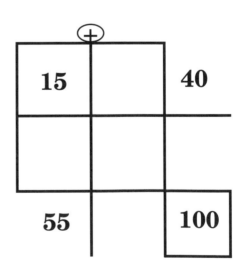

160

Two Ways

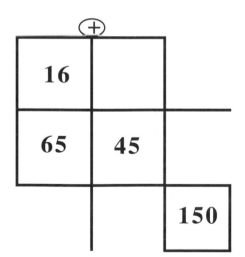

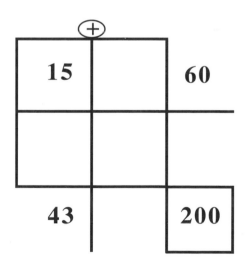

161

Two Ways

(X)

2		8
		16
	32	128

(X)

	27	81
9		243

(X)

12		72
3		360

(X)

4		16
	2	
36		

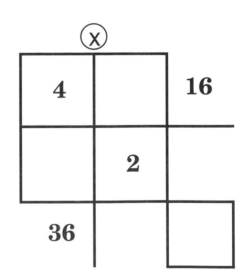

162

Two Ways

	⊗	
8		24

12	288

	⊗	
2		
	16	64
8		256

	⊗	
6		
		20
12		360

	⊗	
3		27
75		675

Two Ways

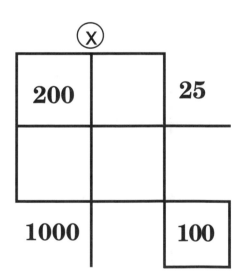

⊗	
24		**12**
6	**36**

⊗	
	48	**6**
16	
	12	

⊗	
	100
80		**20**
8	

⊗	
200		**25**
1000	**100**

164

Two Ways

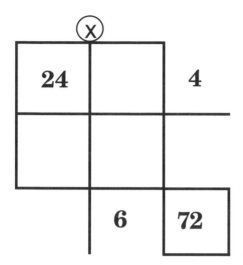

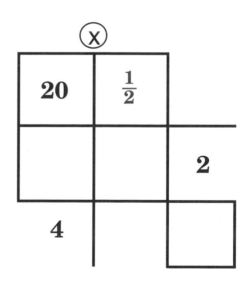

Two Ways

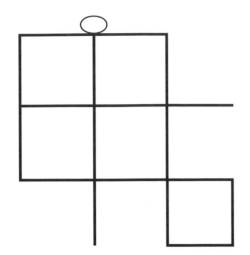

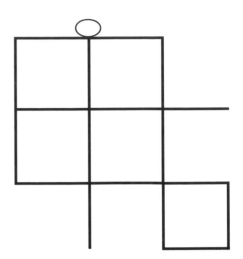

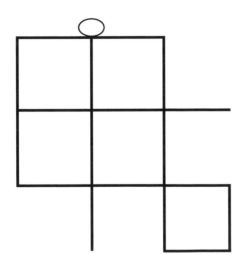

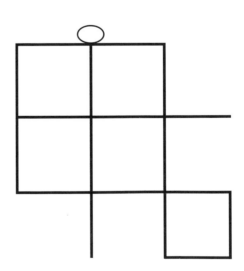

References

Bauersfeld, H. (1980). Hidden dimensions in the so-called reality of a mathematics classroom. *Educational Studies in Mathematics, 11,* 23-41.

Bauersfeld, H. (1996). Social constructivism, classroom cultures and other concepts: What can they mean for teachers? Psychology for Mathematics Education - North American Chapter, Panama City, FL.

Brown, J, S., Collins, A., and Duguid, P. (1989). Situated cognition and the culture of learning. *Educational Researcher, 18(1),* 32-41.

Brown, S. I. and Walter, M. I. (1983). *The art of problem posing.* Philadelphia, PA: Franklin Institute Press.

Cobb, P. (1996). Mathematics learning and small group interaction: Four Case studies. In P. Cobb and H. Bauersfeld, (Eds.), *The emergence of mathematical meaning: Interaction in classrooms cultures.* Hillsdale, NJ: Erlbaum.

Cobb, P. and Bauersfeld, H. Eds. (1995). *The emergence of mathematical meaning: Interaction in classrooms cultures.* Hillsdale, NJ: Erlbaum.

Cobb, P., Wood, T. and Yackel, E. (1992). A constructivist alternative to the representational view of the mind in mathematics education. *Journal for Research in Mathematics Education, 23(1),* 1-33.

Cobb, P., Wood, T., and Yackel, E. (1995). A constructivist approach to second grade mathematics. In E. von Glaserfeld (Ed*.), Radical constructivism in mathematics education.* Dordrecht, Holland: Kluwer.

Cobb, P., Yackel, E. and Merkel, G. and Wheatley, G. (1988). Research into practice: Creating a problem solving atmosphere. *Arithmetic Teacher, 36(1),* 46-47.

Egan, K. (1988*). Teaching as storytelling: An alternative to teaching and the curriculum.* London: Routledge.

Hatano, G. (1979). Learning to add and subtract: A Japanese perspective. In T. Carpenter, J. Moser, & T. Rhomberg (Eds.)*, Addition and subtraction: A cognitive perspective.* Hillsdale, NJ: Lawrence Erlbaum. (pp. 211-223)

Hundeide, K. (1986). Tacit background of children's judgment. In J. V. Wertsch (Ed.), *Culture, communication and cognition: Vygotskian perspective.* London: Cambridge University Press, pp. 306-322.

Kennedy, J. (1993). Problem solving on geoboards. *Mathematics Teacher, 86(1),* 82.

Krutetskii, V. (1976). *The psychology of mathematical abilities in school children.* Chicago: University of Chicago Press.

Kuhn, T. (1970). *Structure of scientific revolutions.* Chicago, IL: The University of Chicago Press.

Lo, J., Wheatley, G. and Smith, A. (1994). The influence of mathematics class discussion on the beliefs and arithmetic meaning of a third grade student. *Journal for Research in Mathematics Education, 25(1),* 30-49.

Mason, J. and Burton, L. (1987). *Thinking mathematically.* New York: Addison Wesley.

National Council of Teachers of Mathematics (1991). *Professional standards for teaching mathematics.* Reston, VA: National Council of Teachers of Mathematics.

Nicholls, J., Cobb, P., Yackel, E., Wood, T., Wheatley, G., Trigatti, B., and Perlwitz, M. (1991). Assessment of a problem centered second-grade mathematics project. *Journal for Research in Mathematics Education, 22(1)*, 3-29.

Pesek, D. and Kirshner, D. (2000). Interference of instrumental instruction in subsequent relational learning. *Journal for Research in Mathematics Education, 31(5)*, 524-540. Polya, G. (1962). *Mathematical discovery: On understanding, learning, and teaching mathematical problem solving.* New York: John Wiley and Sons.

Prawat, R. S. (1993). The value of ideas: Problems versus possibilities. *Educational Researcher*, 5-16.

Reynolds, A. M. and Wheatley, G. H. (1996). Elementary student's construction and coordination of units in an area setting. *Journal for Research in Mathematics Education, 27(5)*, 564-581.

Richards, J. (1991). Mathematical discussions. In E. von Glasersfeld, *Radical constructivism in mathematics education.* Dordrecht, Netherlands: Kluwer Academic Publishers.

Schmidt, W. McKnight, C and Raizen, S. (1990). *A Splintered Vision: An Investigation of U.S. Science and Mathematics Education.* Dordrecht/Boston/London: Kluwer Academic Publishers.

Sfard, A. (1994). Reification as the birth of metaphor. *For the Learning of Mathematics, 14(1)*, 44-55.

Sfard, A. (2000). Steering (dis)course between metaphors and rigor: Using focal analysis to investigate an emergence of mathematical objects. *Journal for Research in Mathematics Education, 31*(3), 296-327.

Smith, John P. III. (1997). Problems with problematizing mathematics: A reply to Hiebert et al. *Educational Researcher, 26(2)*. 22-24.

Steffe, L. (1990). Adaptive Mathematics Teaching. In T. Cooney and C. Hirsch (Eds.), *Teaching mathematics in the 1990s.* Reston VA: National Council of Teachers of Mathematics.

Steffe, L. (1993). Interactions and children's mathematics. Paper presented at the annual meeting of the American Educational Research Association, Atlanta, GA.

Steffe, L. , von Glasersfeld, E., Richards, J. and Cobb, P. (1983*). Children's counting types: Philosophy, theory, and application.* New York: Praeger Scientific.

Steffe, L. P. (1991). The constructivist teaching experiment: Illustrations and implications. In Glasersfeld, E. von (Ed.) *Radical constructivism in mathematics education.* Boston: Kluwer Academic.

Trowell, S. and Wheatley, G. (1994). Establishing an effective learning environment in a mathematics classroom. Paper presented at the Annual meeting of the International Group for the Psychology of Mathematics Education, Lisbon, Portugal.

Varela, F. J., Thompson, E. and Rosch, E. (1993). *The embodied mind: Cognitive science and human experience.* Cambridge, MA: The MIT Press.

von Glasersfeld, E. (1987). *The construction of knowledge: Contributions to conceptual semantics.* Salinas, CA: Intersystems Publications.

Wheatley, G. H. (1991). Constructivist perspectives on mathematics and science learning. *Science Education, 75(1)*, 9-21.

Wheatley, G. H. (1996). *Quick draw: Developing spatial sense in mathematics.* Tallahassee, FL: Mathematics Learning.

Wheatley, G. H. and Reynolds, A. M. (1996). The construction of abstract units in geometric and numerical settings. *Educational Studies in Mathematics, 30*, 67- 83.

Wheatley, G. H. and Wheatley, C. L. (1982). Calculator use and problem solving strategies of grade six pupils. Final report submitted to the National Science Foundation. ERIC Number ED219250.

Wirtz, R. (1980). *New beginnings*. Monterey, CA: Curriculum Development Associates.

Wood, T. and Sellers, P. (1996). Assessment of a problem-centered mathematics program: Third grade. *Journal for Research in Mathematics Education, 27(3),* 337-353.

Yackel, E. and Cobb, P. (1996). Sociomathematical norms, argumentation, and autonomy in mathematics. *Journal for Research in Mathematics Education, 27(4),* 458-477.

Appendix A

Problem Sets

Problem Solving I

1. Tina had some candies. She gave 4 to Carlos. Then she had 8 left. How many candies did she have at first?

2. There are 24 pencils. Mrs. Leonard wants to share them fairly with 8 children. How many pencils will each child get?

3. At the zoo Patty saw 15 lions and tigers. There were three more lions than tigers. How many were tigers?

4. We have 12 square tables, each of which seats 1 person on a side. If we push them together to form one long table, how many people can be seated?

5. Each flashlight uses two batteries. Pat has 5 batteries. How many more batteries are needed for 4 flashlights?

6. In a field there were horses and ducks. When Tom looked through the fence he could see 5 heads and 14 legs. How many horses were there? How many ducks?

7. I am thinking of two numbers. When I add them I get 13. When I subtract them I get 3. What are the two numbers?

8. I am thinking of two numbers that add to 12. One of them is the double of the other. What are the two numbers?

9. How can you make 37 cents with seven coins?

10. I have 21 cents. How many coins could I have? Find them all!

11. How many wheels altogether on 4 bicycles and four tricycles?

12. How many wheels altogether on three cars and three bicycles?

13. How many wheels on 5 cars, 5 bicycles, and 5 tricycles?

14. I have some pennies, nickels and dimes in my pocket. If I put 3 coins in my hand, how much money could I have in my hand?

15. I am thinking of a number. I add 7 and then subtract 3. I now have 9. What is my number?

16. Eleven children got on the bus. There were five more girls than boys. How many of each were there?

17. Alisha had 19 M&Ms. She ate seven and shared the rest equally with Paula. How many M&Ms did Paula get?

18. Debbie has 40 books to stack on shelves. Each shelf will hold 11 books. What is the smallest number of shelves she will need?

19. Shasha's big dog eats 3 cups of food each day. How many days will 19 cups last?

20. I am thinking of a number. If I take half of it and add 3 I get 11. What is the number?

21. I am thinking of a number. If I double it and subtract 5 I get 11. What is the number?

Problem Solving II (multiplication and division)

The tasks below are meant to be illustrative of problem and format types.

1. $2 \times 8 = \underline{\quad}$

2. $6 \times \underline{\quad} = 30$

3. $\underline{\quad} \times 7 = 21$

4. $24 = 8 \times \underline{\quad}$

5. $40 \div 8 = \underline{\quad}$

6. $26 \times 10 = \underline{\quad}$

7. $10 \times \underline{\quad} = 210$

8. How many sixes are needed to make 24?

9. How many threes in 21?

10. Each pack of baseball cards has four cards in it. You have 24 cards. How many more packs do you need to have 40 cards?

11. Antwon was planting trees in rows. Each row had the same number of trees. He planted 28 trees. How many trees in each row?

12. A floor in the shape of a square is covered with 16 square tiles. There are four tiles on one side. How many tiles on each of the other sides?

13. Six bags of cookies each have five cookies in it. How many cookies altogether?

14. A school has five teams with nine players on each team. How many players in all"

15. A bookcase has four shelves. There are the same number of books on each shelf. There are 36 books on the shelves. How many books on each shelf?

Stacking Cards

1. Chan was making stacks of baseball cards. He wanted 9 in each stack. How many stacks would there be with 36 cards? 45 cards?

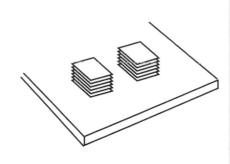

2. Suppose he wanted to make 12 stacks with 60 cards. How many cards would be in each stack?

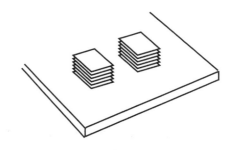

3. After making six stacks of nine cards each, Chan added more cards to make seven stacks with ten cards in each stack. How many MORE cards did he use?

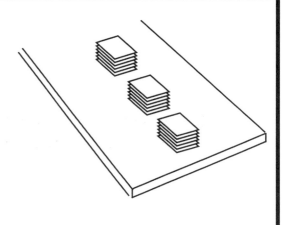

Stacking Cans

1. Roberto was stacking soda cans on a shelf at the store where he worked. He could stack five cans high and seven cans across the front. How many cans could he stack in the front?

2. Later, Roberto was asked to stack cans six high and eight across. How many MORE cans could he stack?

3. Roberto could also stack the cans four deep on the shelf. He stacked six high and eight across. How many cans could he stack?

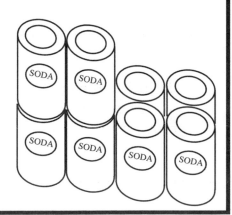

Packing Boxes

1. Jose was packing boxes in cartons. He could just fit five rows of four boxes on the first layer. How many boxes could he put on this layer?

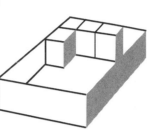

2. Marta needed to pack 30 boxes in a carton. Five boxes would fit in each row. How many rows would there be?

3. Marta had another carton. She could pack 24 boxes in this carton. How many rows could there be?

4. In a larger carton Marta could pack five rows of four on the bottom and stack the boxes three high. How many boxes could she put in the carton?

Tiles

1. Sara laid our square tiles with seven across
    and five high. How many tiles did she use?

    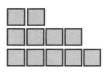

2. Suppose she had five tiles across and seven
    high. How many MORE rows of five would
    she need to add to have 50 tiles?

3. Sara had four rows of tiles with six tiles in each
    row. If she wanted to have a seven by five set
    of tiles, how many tiles should she add?

4. Sara had six rows of blue tiles with four in each
    row. She added a border of white tiles at the
    top and on one side. How many white tiles did
    she add?

Gameboards

1. Jennifer made a gameboard which had six rows with five squares in each row. How many squares would there be on the gameboard?

2. Kim made a gameboard with ten squares in each row. If she wanted to have seventy squares, how many rows would she need?

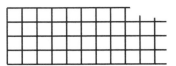

3. Kim decided she wanted the gameboard to have two more rows with two more squares in each row. How many MORE squares would this new gameboard have?

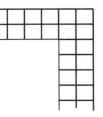

4. A checker board has eight rows with eight squares in each row. How many squares are there on a checkerboard?

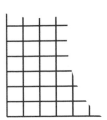

Appendix B
Mathematical Games

Mathematics Games

The purpose of engaging children in games is not drill and practice but the opportunity to make numbers meaningful. Game situations facilitate this sense making. In selecting games, analyze play to look for opportunities for constructing patterns and relationships. In addition to the games included in this volume, consider the following commercial games.

War, Double War

Piggy Bank

Card games

Concentration

Dominoes

Combo-Ten – Fosters thinking in tens

Parcheesi, Double Parcheesi

Racko - Builds an ordinal sense of number

Sorry

Checkers, Backgammon, Chess

Yhatzee

Mastermind – Builds logical reasoning

For a collection of other mathematics games designed for elementary students see

Kamii, C. K. (1985). *Young children reinvent arithmetic: Implications of Piaget's theory*. New York: Teachers College Press.

Quick Dot

Tell the students you will show them a card with dots on it and you want them to tell you how many there are and how they see them. Show them the card (3 seconds). Ask students how many dots they saw and how they saw them. As students share their responses, encourage all answers. Repeat the activity with other dot cards—15 minutes.

Sample Questions
What did you see? How many did you see?
How were they arranged? How did you see them?
What did the look like? Did anyone see anything different?

Materials
Overhead Projector, Dot pattern overhead transparencies

Instructional Strategy
Teacher directed discussion.

Assessment
As students explain what they saw in looking at the dot cards, you will get a good sense of their number development. Afterwards, make anecdotal records of student's responses.

Extension _
Choosing more challenging dot cards and having students draw what they see (in their journals) can easily extend this activity.

Variatiations
To make the task more concrete allows students to use counters to show what they've seen. You might also, at times, have students draw what they saw.

Sample dot pattern cards

  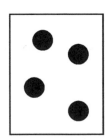 

Sample dialogue

"I am going to show you a pattern of dots. I want you to decide how many dots they are. Ready?" The teacher shows the following dot arrangements for three seconds. After time for students to think, she gives them a second look.

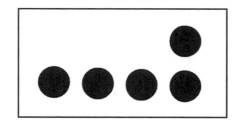

Teacher:	Tell me how many you saw and how you saw them.
Cathy:	I saw 5.
Teacher:	Keith saw 5. How were they arranged?
Cathy:	I saw 4 and 1 on top.
Teacher:	Does anybody see it differently?
Pat:	I saw 6 and they looked like an L.
Teacher:	Pat, explain what the L looked like.
Pat:	It was lying on its side and the top part had 1 dot. There were 5 on the bottom part.
Kelly:	Pat, I think there's only 4 on the bottom and 1 on the top.
Teacher:	Pat, would you like another look? (T shows dots again and leaves it in View.
Arleshia:	I saw three across and two up. Three and two are five.
Convay:	Yeah, that's how I saw it too—five dots.

Where Is the Mathematics?

Working with dot patterns can help students think in collections rather than just number names in the counting sequence. Students frequently see arrangements of objects but do not always "make" them a collection. After this lesson they may see four dinner plates as a set of four rather thathan just four separate things. This leads to the development of powerful strategies for adding and subtracting. In this activity, students can build mental images of numbers. When they hear or see six, an image of six dots arranged in some manner can be evoked.

Dot Pattern Cards

Goal: Develop mental images for numbers
      Thinking in collections
       Beginning addition

Activity 1
Have each student select and display on desk the cards six through ten.
Show a three card and a six card. Ask students to "Hold up one of your cards which has the same number of dots as these cards." Repeat with other pairs of cards.

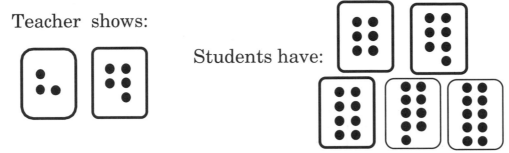

Activity 2
Have students display on their desk the dot cards two through six.
Show a seven card and ask, "Hold up two of your cards which have the same number of dots as this one."

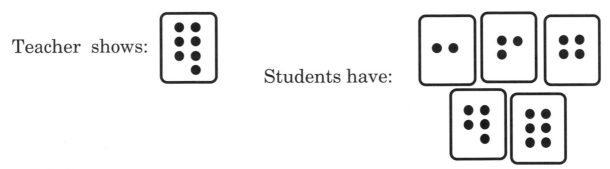

Activity 3
Have students display on their desk the dot cards two through six.
Show the two card. Ask, "What card can we put with this one to make seven?" Repeat with different numbers.

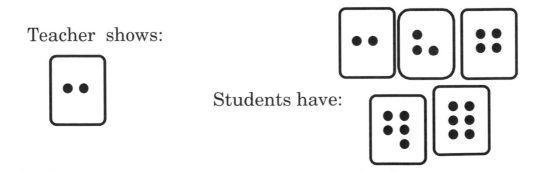

192

Where is the mathematics?

While counting provides many opportunities for building number patterns, many students come to rely on it as a rote procedure for finding how many or how many are left. Working with dot patterns can help students think in collections rather than simply counting by ones which leads to powerful number patterns and strategies for adding and subtracting.

In this activity students can build mental images of numbers. When they hear or see six, an image of six dots arranged in some manner can be evoked. In this way, six can come to have a richer meaning. It is important for students to have other ways of adding and subtracting than counting-on. Memorization of facts without the imagery can be detrimental in that it tends to discourage building of patterns and relationships.

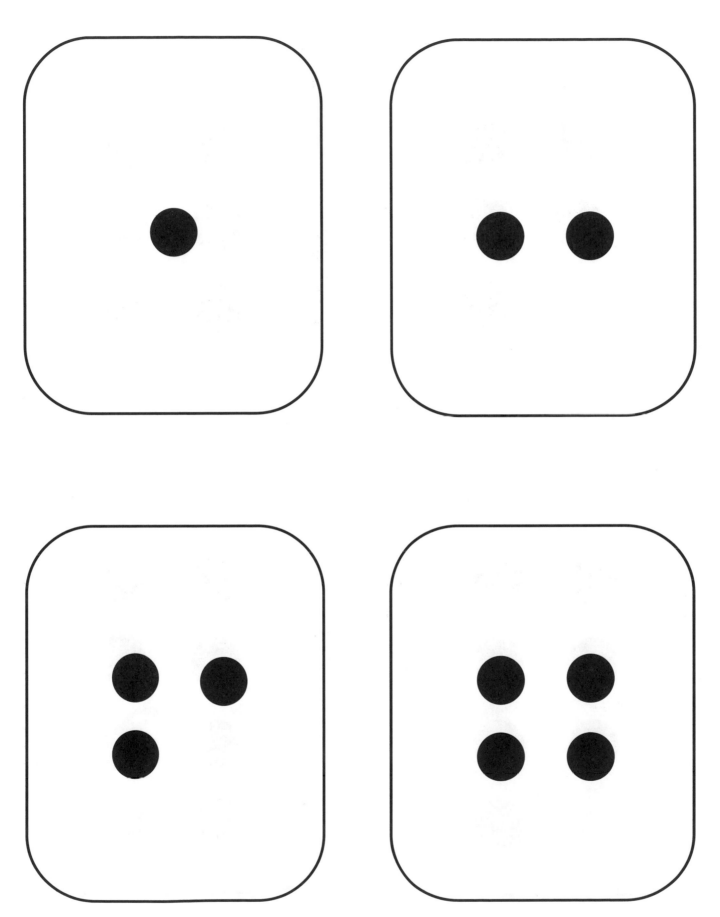

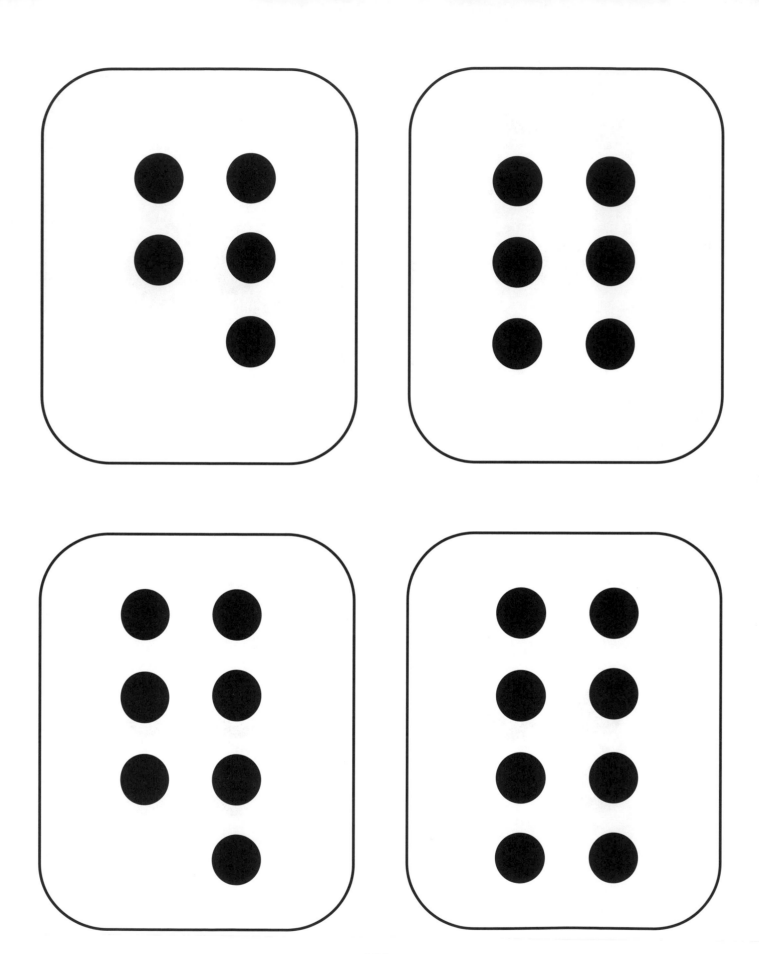

196

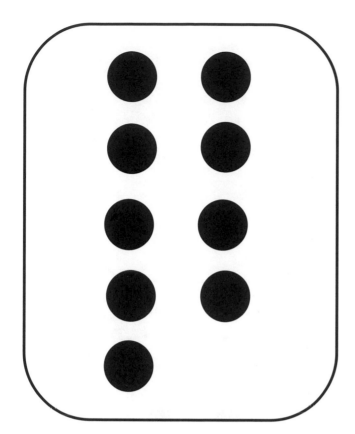

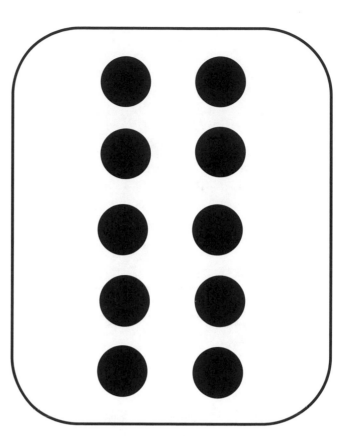

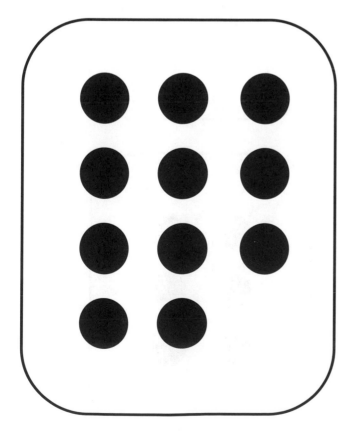

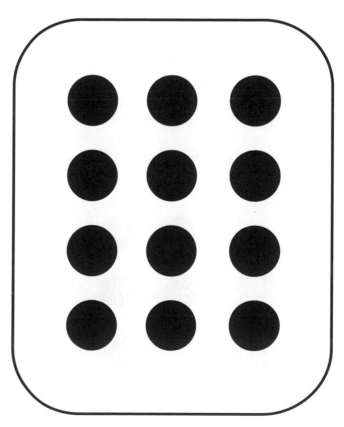

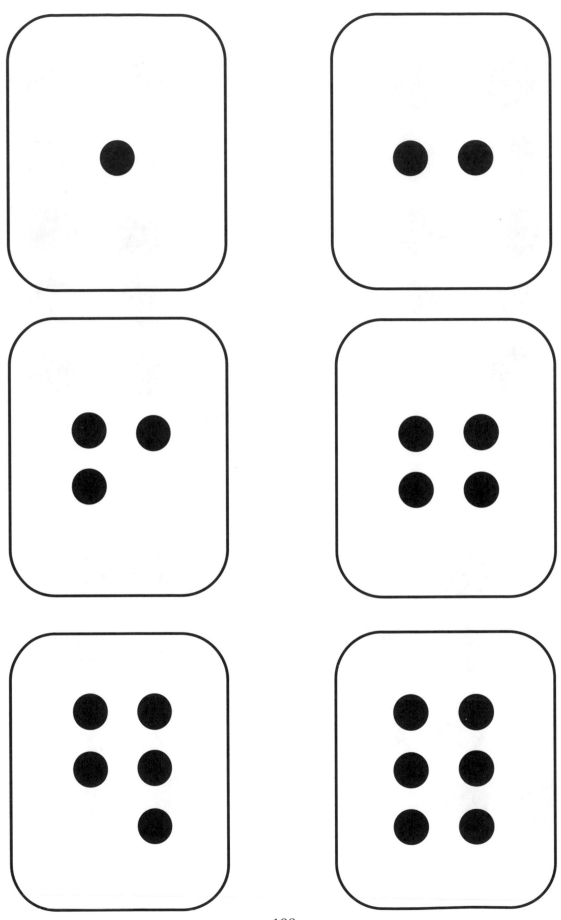

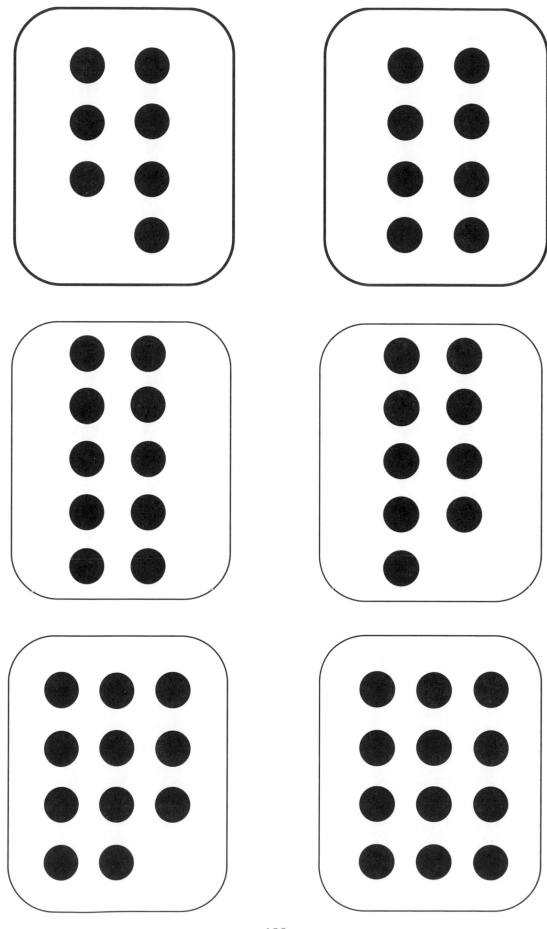

Dot Pattern Match

The Dot Pattern Match Game cards on the four sheets that follow can be cutout and laminated. These cards are used to help students construct mental images of numbers and learn larger and smaller.

Materials
One deck of cards contains:
Two pairs of twos, threes, fours, fives, sixes, and sevens, and three pairs of eights,

The Match Game
Students play in pairs.
Have students lay out the 30 cards face down in a 5 by 6 array on the floor (they won't fit on a desk). Students take turns turning over two cards. If a player turns over two cards that match, he or she takes those two cards, otherwise the cards are turned back over in the same location trying to remember the number of dots on that card. The next player does the same and play continues until all cards have been removed. The student with the most cards is the winner.

Variation: For less advanced players you may want to reduce the number of cards by taking out some of the higher numbered pairs. For example, you might use only 12 cards (six pairs).

The High Card Game
Students play in pairs.
The cards are shuffled and dealt out evenly, fifteen to each person. The players each turn over a card at the same time. The one with the higher card takes the two cards. If the two cards have the same number of dots then they are left and the pile builds. After all cards have been turned over, the one with the most cards wins.

Where is the Mathematics?
Students have an opportunity to construct mental images for the numbers one through eight. Because the arrangement of dots for the same number varies, their images can become more abstract. Students can also develop additive reasoning as they play this game. A student might not initially recognize "eight" as the total number of dots on a card she turns over; however she has an opportunity to recognize patterns of smaller numbers within the arrangement of eight dots and combine those to make eight - five dots and three dots, for example.

What you as teacher can learn
You can learn much by watching how your students decide if two cards match (or if one is a higher number for the alternate game). Note which students decide on a match by simply "looking" at the cards. This suggests

they have constructed mental images for the numbers. Some students may pause for a short time, examining the cards without appearing to count the dots, before they decide. Take time to ask these students how they decided if the cards were a match. You might find that these students have not yet developed images for larger numbers like 6, 7, or 8 but may be looking for smaller number arrangements that they can use for comparison. For example, in deciding if cards with 7 and 8 dots displayed are the same or different, students have been observed making a "four" on each card and then noticing that they have 4 dots remaining on one card and 3 on the other, hence not a match. These students are using thinking strategies to help them decide how many and make a comparison. You might notice some students counting the dots to determine how many on a card. This is a flag that these students have not yet constructed mental images for the numbers. The Quick Flash of ten frames and double ten frames and the Spot the Dot activities are designed to encourage these students to construct mental images for these numbers. In this setting, the students learn to use mental images and transformations rather than counting in finding out how many.

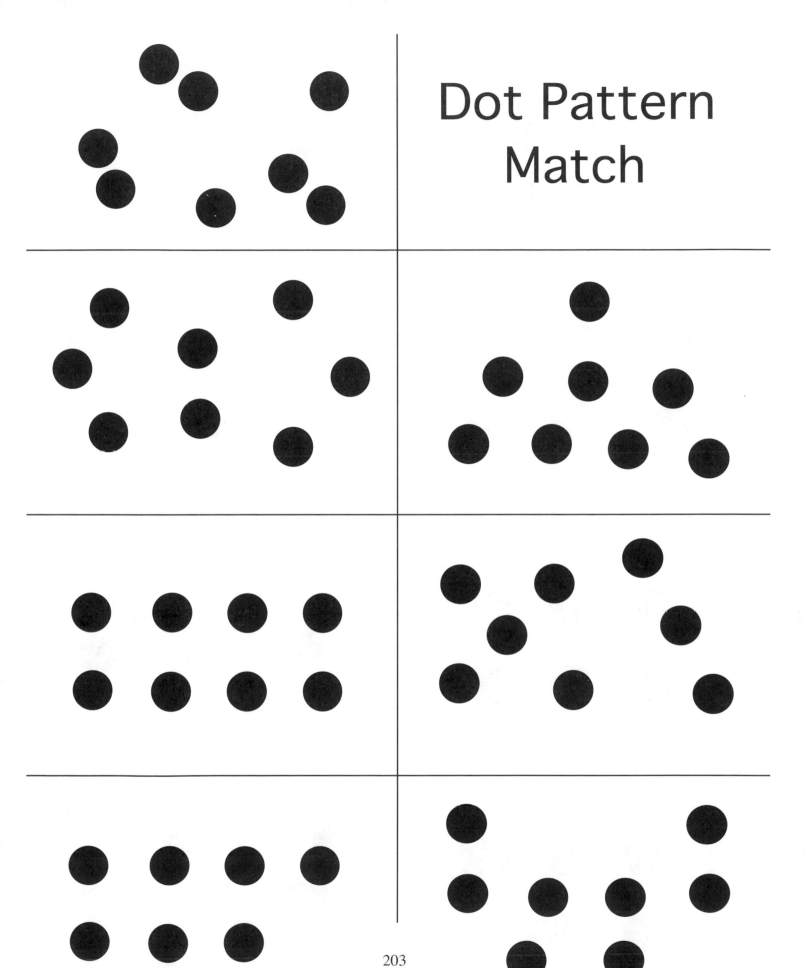

Dot Pattern
Match

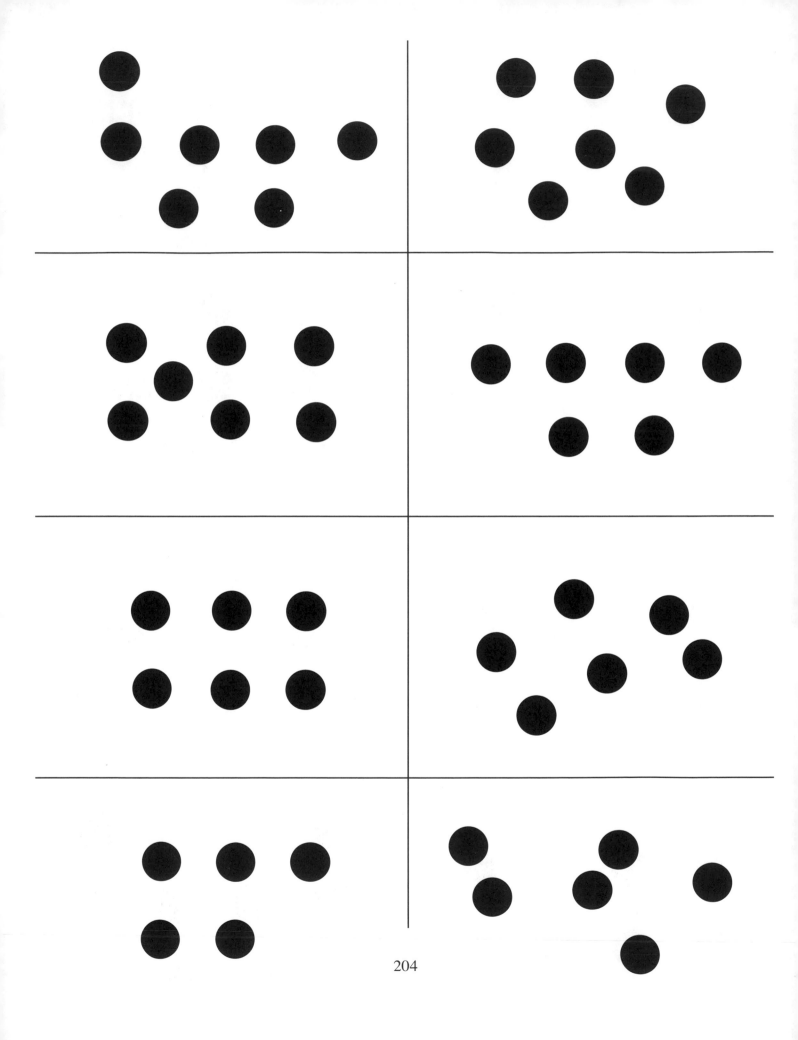

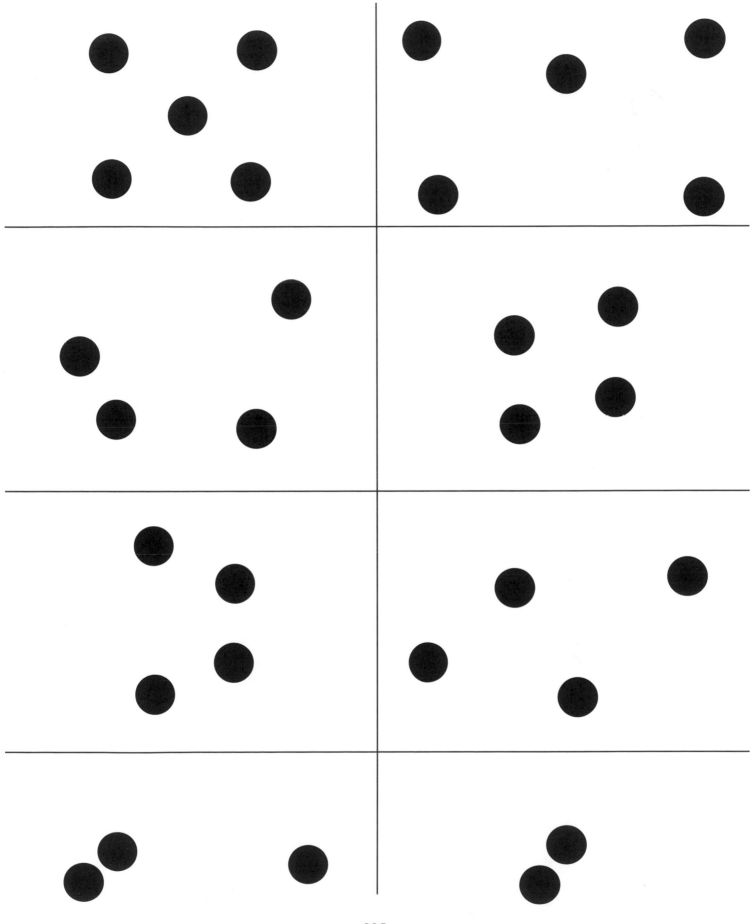

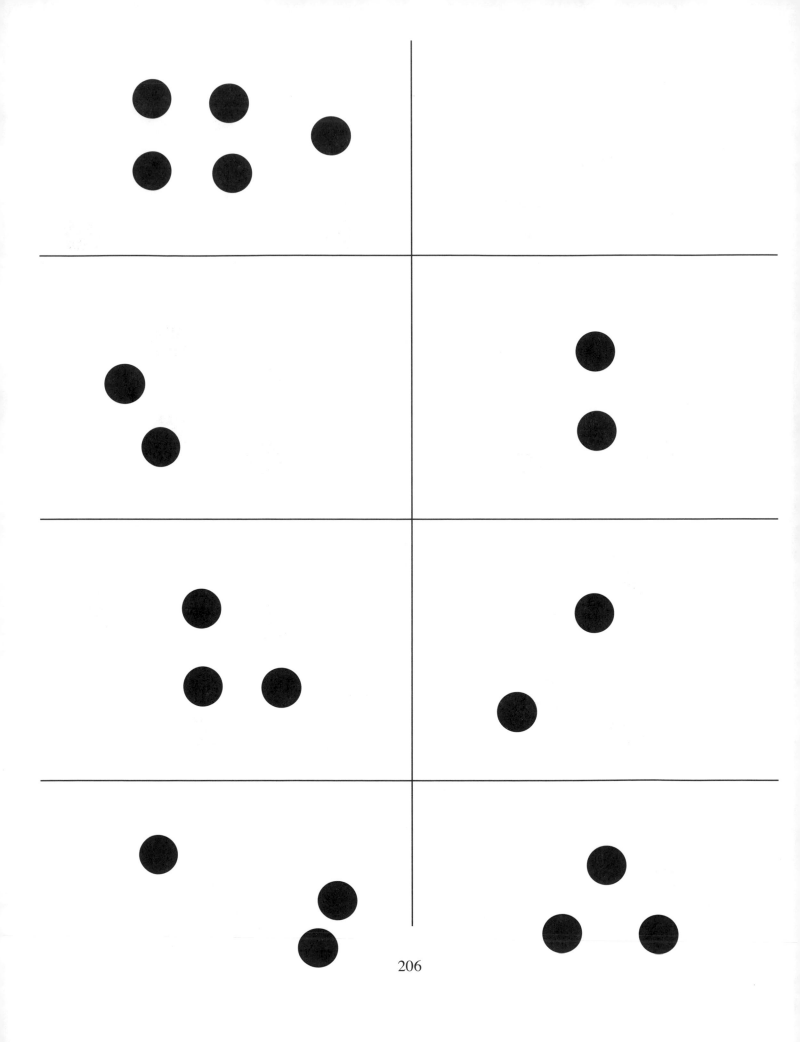

206

Ten Frame Match

The Dot Pattern Match Game cards on the four sheets that follow can be cutout and laminated. These cards are used to help students construct mental images of numbers and learn larger and smaller.

Materials
One deck of cards contains:
Two pairs of twos, threes, fours,
fives, sixes, and sevens,
and three pairs of eights,

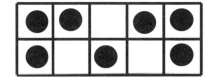

The Match Game
Students play in pairs.
Have students lay out the 30 cards face down in a 5 by 6 array on the floor (they won't fit on a desk). Students take turns turning over two cards. If a player turns over two cards that match, he or she takes those two cards, otherwise the cards are turned back over in the same location trying to remember the number of dots on that card. The next player does the same and play continues until all cards have been removed. The student with the most cards is the winner.

Variation: For less advanced players you may want to reduce the number of cards by taking out some of the higher numbered pairs. For example, you might use only 12 cards (six pairs).

The High Card Game
Students play in pairs.
The cards are shuffled and dealt out evenly, fifteen to each person. The players each turn over a card at the same time. The one with the higher card takes the two cards. If the two cards have the same number of dots then they are left and the pile builds. After all cards have been turned over, the one with the most cards wins.

Where is the Mathematics?
Students have an opportunity to construct mental images for the numbers one through eight. Because the arrangement of dots for the same number varies, their images can become more abstract. Students can also develop additive reasoning as they play this game. A student might not initially recognize "eight" as the total number of dots on a card she turns over; however she has an opportunity to recognize patterns of smaller numbers within the arrangement of eight dots and combine those to make eight - five dots and three dots, for example.

What you as teacher can learn
You can learn much by watching how your students decide if two cards match (or if one is a higher number for the alternate game). Note which students decide on a match by simply "looking" at the cards. This suggests

they have constructed mental images for the numbers. Some students may pause for a short time, examining the cards without appearing to count the dots, before they decide. Take time to ask these students how they decided if the cards were a match. You might find that these students have not yet developed images for larger numbers like 6, 7, or 8 but may be looking for smaller number arrangements that they can use for comparison. For example, in deciding if cards with 7 and 8 dots displayed are the same or different, students have been observed making a "four" on each card and then noticing that they have 4 dots remaining on one card and 3 on the other, hence not a match. These students are using thinking strategies to help them decide how many and make a comparison. You might notice some students counting the dots to determine how many on a card. This is a flag that these students have not yet constructed mental images for the numbers. The Quick Flash of ten frames and double ten frames and the Spot the Dot activities are designed to encourage these students to construct mental images for these numbers. In this setting, the students learn to use mental images and transformations rather than counting in finding out how many.

Ten Frame Match

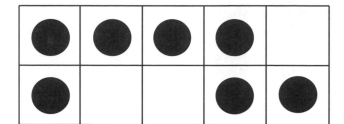

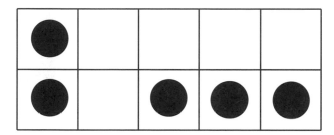

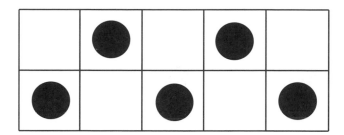

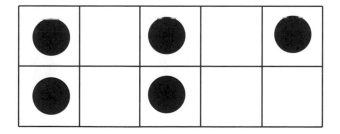

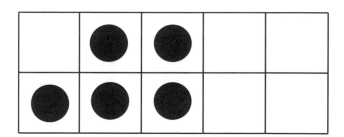

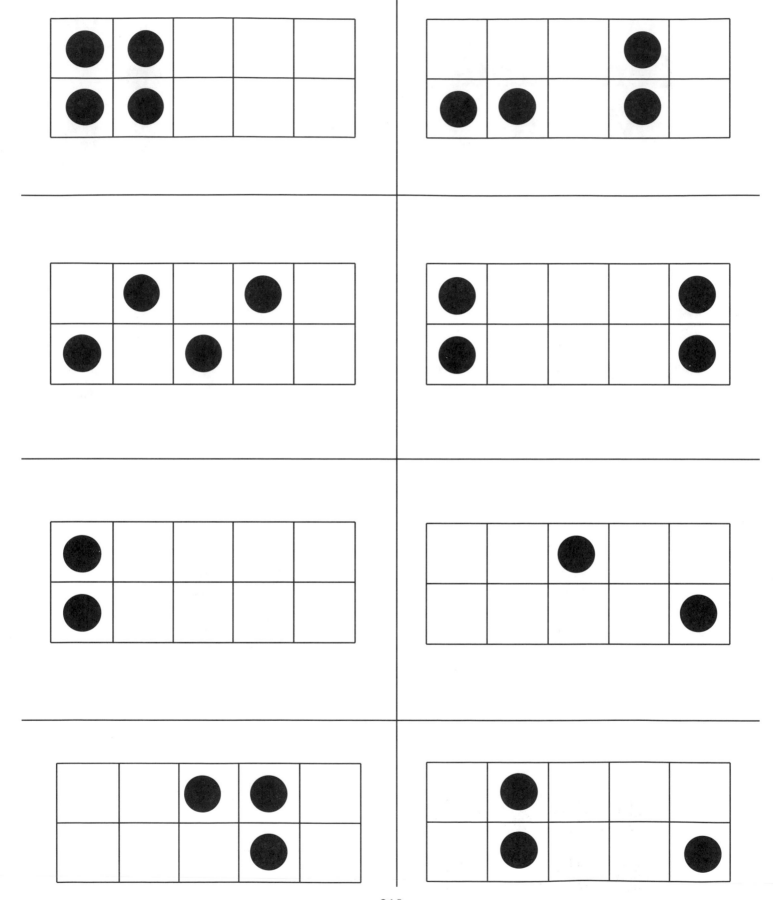

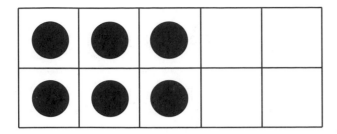

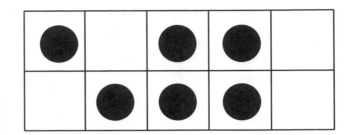

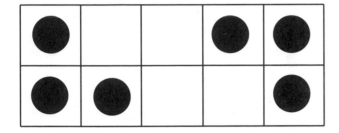

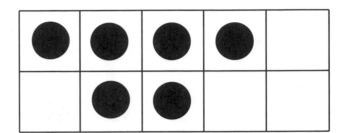

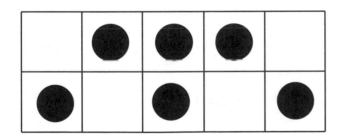

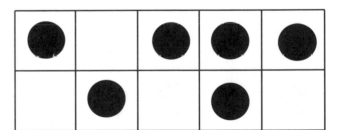

211

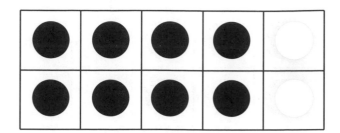

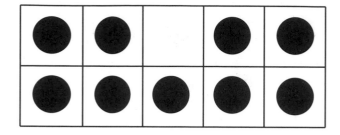

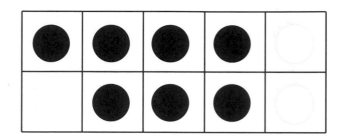

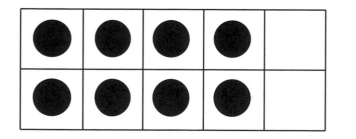

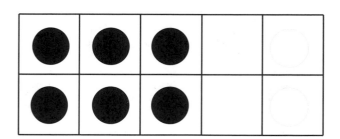

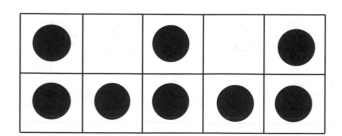

Match Ten

The Match Ten Cards on the four sheets that follow can be cutout and laminated. The cards are used to help students construct ten as an abstract (mental) mathematical object.

Materials:
One deck of cards contains:
one pair of 0 and 10, two pairs of 1 and 9,
two pairs of 2 and 8, four pairs of 3 and 7,
four pairs of 4 and 6, and
two pairs of 5 and 5.

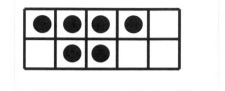

The Concentration Game
Students play in pairs.
Have students lay out the 30 cards face down in a 5 by 6 array on the floor (they won't fit on a desk). Students take turns turning over two cards. If the pair makes ten, they take the two cards, otherwise they turn them back over in the same location trying to remember the number of dots on that card. The next player does the same and play continues until all cards have been removed. The student with the most cards is the winner.

Variation: For less advanced players you may want to reduce the number of cards by taking out some of the ten-pairs. For example, you might use only 12 cards (six pairs).

The Match Game
Another way of using Match Ten cards in the classroom is to distribute one card to each student. You then show a card and the students who have a card that makes ten with yours holds it up. Students can also play this way in a small group. The cards can be used in a wide variety of ways.

Where is the Mathematics?
Match Ten was designed to provide opportunities for students to think in tens. Since ten is the basis of our numeration system, being able to think of ten in many ways is important. As students play Match Ten, they come to know the combinations which make ten which then helps in adding and subtracting. As students play the game, they are building mental images of numbers from one to ten that they can draw upon in many mathematical situations. The ten frame structures the dots so the mental image is easier to construct and remember. The cards show various arrangements of dots for each number from one through ten.

What you as teacher can learn
You can learn much by watching your students respond. Note how students are determining which card to pick up. Note which students pick up the correct card by just looking at it. This suggests they have previously constructed mental images for the numbers. Other students may count to determine how many dots there are on a card.

Match
Ten

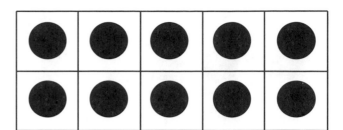

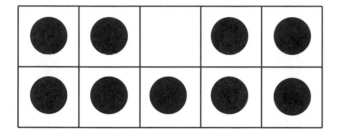

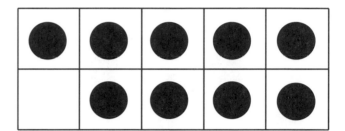

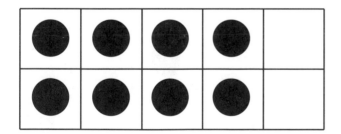

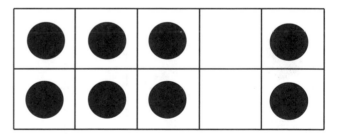

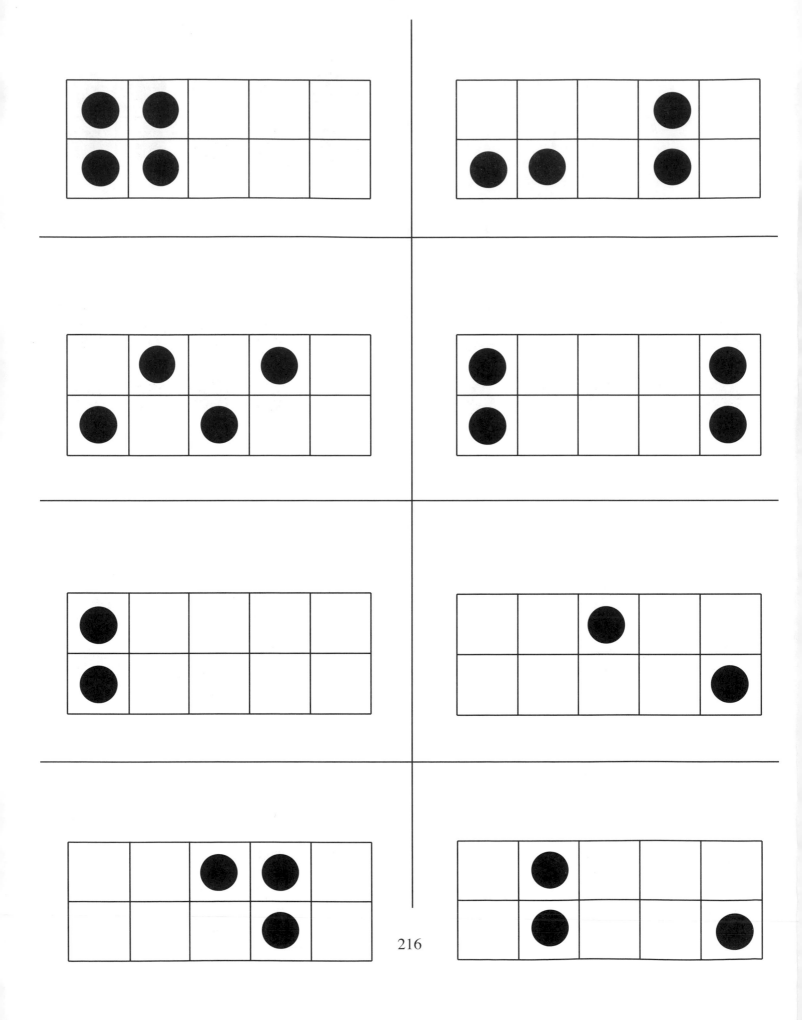

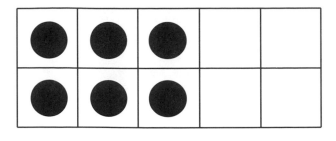

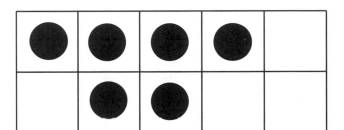

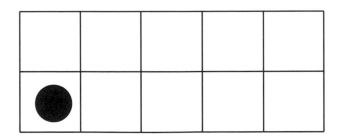

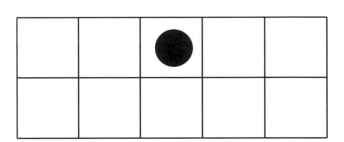

217

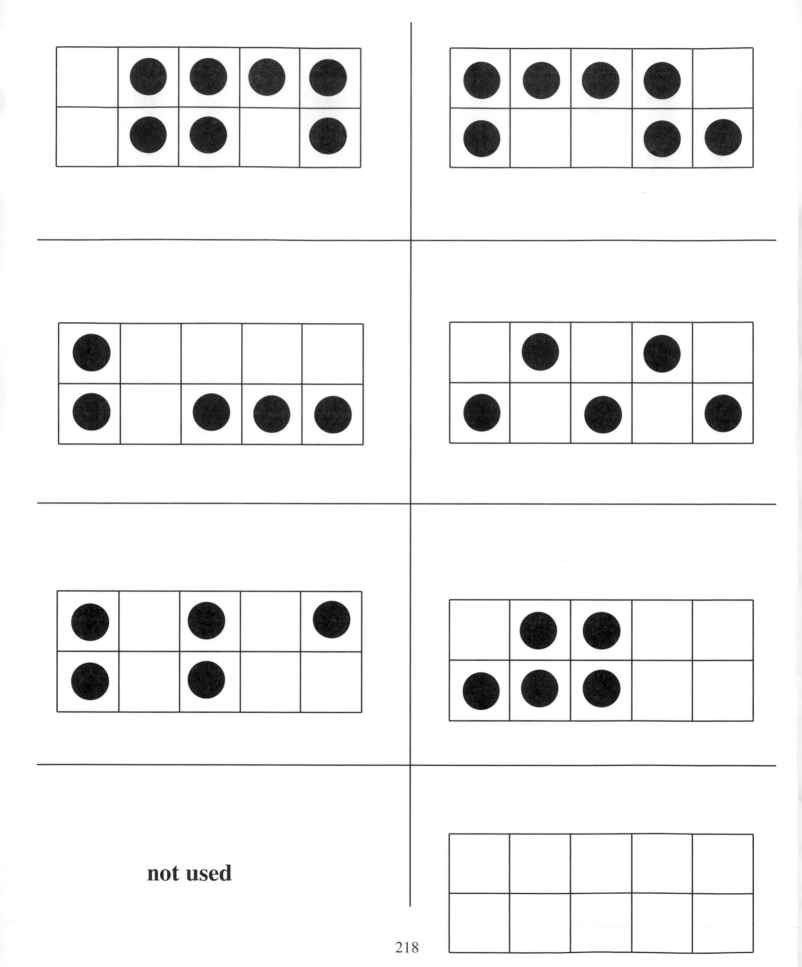

not used

COMBO-TEN

Combo-Ten is an engaging mathematics game similar to dominoes. The set of Combo-Ten pieces provided are designed to facilitate thinking in tens and understanding even and odd numbers. Notice that the dots are arranged in two columns. It the two columns are the same, the number is even. If they are not the same, the number is odd. With the dots arranged in two columns, students can see how two numbers "fit" to make a ten (two rows of five). The normal rules for dominoes can be used with a Combo-Ten set and would be good to use before playing Combo-Ten.

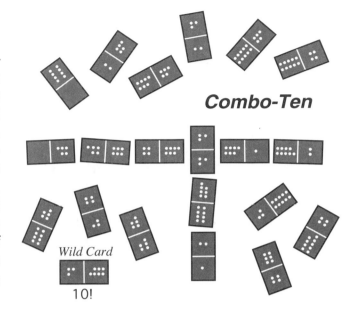

Combo-Ten

Wild Card

10!

GOALS: 1) Encourage the construction of ten as an meaningful unit.
2) Develop strategies for mentally adding whole numbers.

Number of players: Two, three or four.

To play the game:
You will need one Combo-Ten set for each group of students.
Combo-Ten pieces are laid face down and each person draws seven. The other pieces form a "draw pile."
To begin the game, the person with the highest double (or most dots if no one has a double) lays that piece on the table.
A piece can be played if the number of dots on one side of it add to ten with one side of a piece already played.

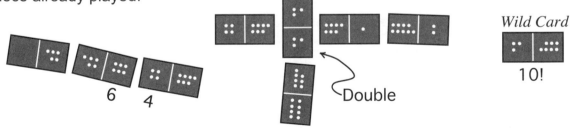

6   4

Wild Card

10!

Double

Doubles are laid sideways and plays can be made off the ends as well as the sides.
A person who cannot play must draw from the pile until a piece is drawn that will play.
The first person to play all their Combo-Ten pieces is the winner.

Wild Cards
A major feature of Combo-Ten is the use of wild cards. If the two numbers on a particular piece add to ten, it is a wild card and can be played at any time. For example, if you need a three and have a (4, 6) piece it can be played as a three. Thus, students will be adding the numbers on each piece they have (or draw) to see if the two numbers add to ten. In this way, students quickly come to know their addition facts to ten.

219

Combo-Ten

A major goal of early school mathematics is thinking in tens. Number sense is founded on a good knowledge of tens and the role they play in our numbers system. Yet, many conventional texts continue to emphasize procedures that lack meaning for young minds. Rather than naming the digit in the tens place, it is much more fruitful to encourage students to look for combinations of ten. Forming the intention of making tens is a singular factor in mental arithmetic. For example, adding 16 and 14 is almost instantaneous when looking for combinations of ten. In fact, it is not necessary for students to memorize addition facts with sums from ten to twenty since all can be determined by making tens. 8 + 5 is 13 because 8 + 2 + 3. Number sense, a central goal, is based on thinking in tens. Combo-Ten is a game that builds mathematical competency by presenting opportunities for students to think in tens.

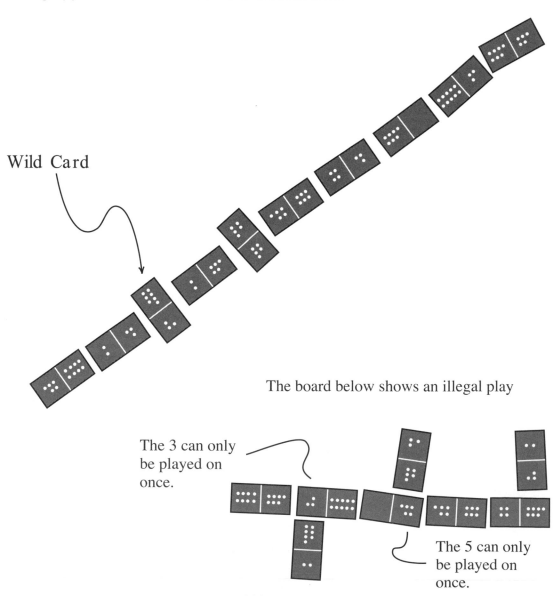

Wild Card

The board below shows an illegal play

The 3 can only be played on once.

The 5 can only be played on once.

220

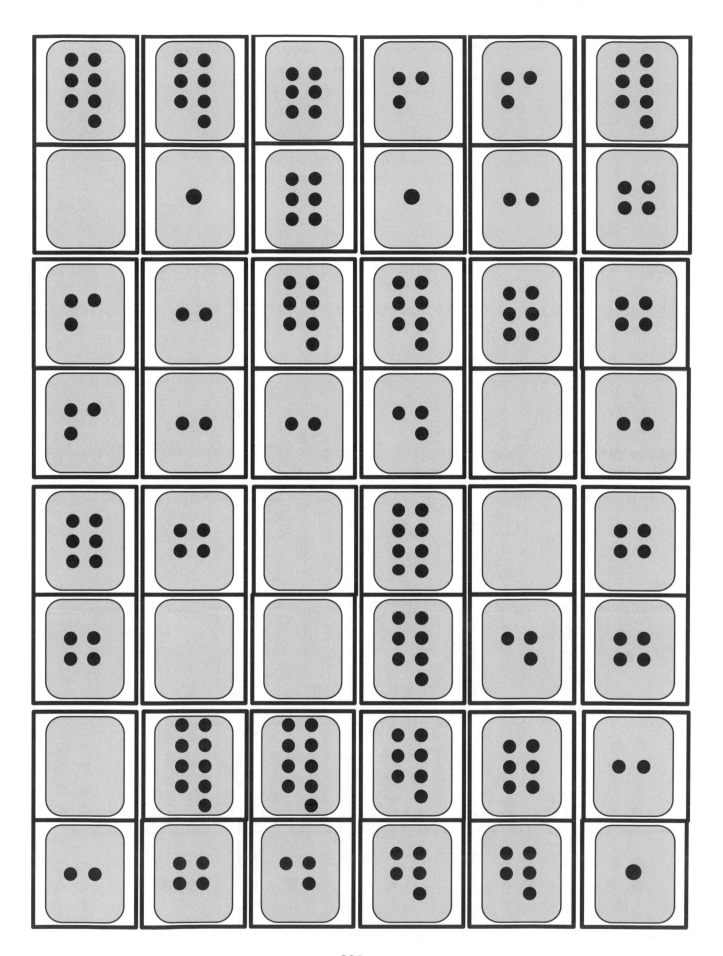

221

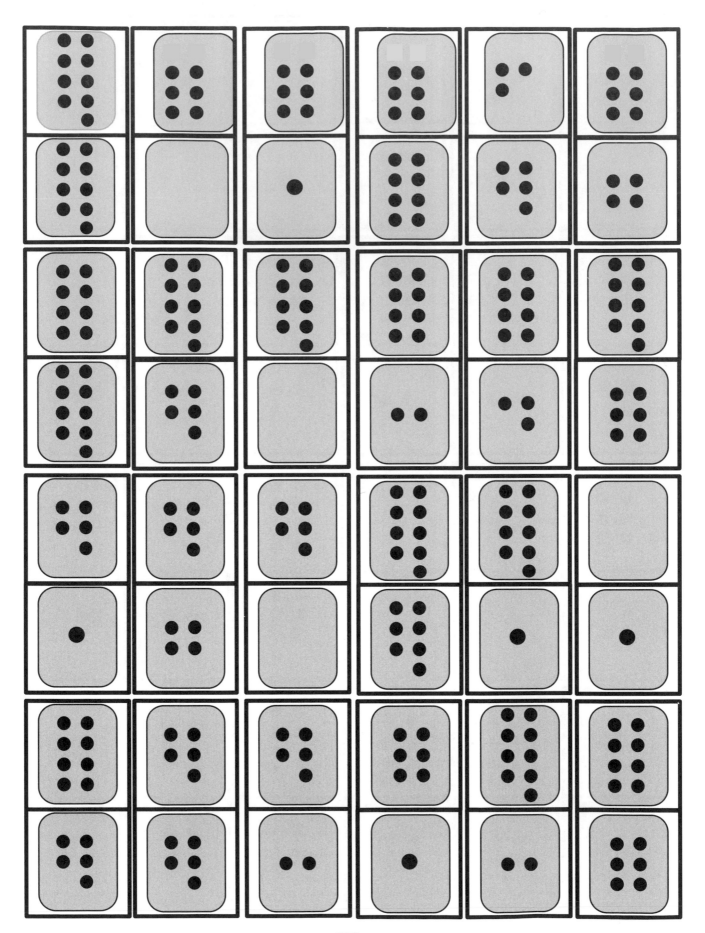

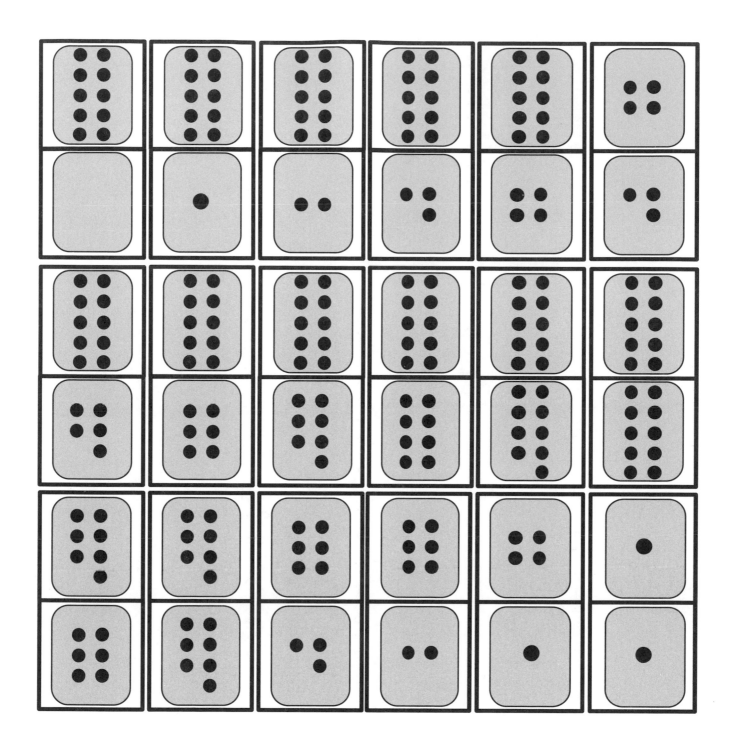